ART OF *I*TALIAN REGIONAL COOKING

*F*rancesco *A*ntonucci
*M*arta *P*ulini
*G*ianni *S*alvaterra

Sterling Publishing Co., Inc.   New York

To our friends whose names begin with the letter A

Library of Congress Cataloging-in-Publication Data

Antonucci, Francesco.
   [Sapore della memoria. English]
   Art of Italian regional cooking / by Francesco Antonucci, Marta
Pulini, and Gianni Salvaterra.
     p.   cm.
   Translation of: Il sapore della memoria.
   Includes index.
   ISBN 0-8069-0849-1
   1. Cookery, Italian. I. Pulini, Marta. II. Salvaterra, Gianni.
III. Title.
   TX723.A58313 1995
   641.5945—dc20   94–45007
                                           CIP

10 9 8 7 6 5 4 3 2 1

Published 1995 by Sterling Publishing Company, Inc.
387 Park Avenue South, New York, N.Y. 10016
Originally published in Italian by Edizioni il Fenicottero
under the title *Il Sapore della Memoria*
© 1993 by Edizioni il Fenicottero
English translation © 1995 by Sterling Publishing Co., Inc.
Distributed in Canada by Sterling Publishing
% Canadian Manda Group, One Atlantic Avenue, Suite 105
Toronto, Ontario, Canada M6K 3E7
Distributed in Great Britain and Europe by Cassell PLC
Villiers House, 41/47 Strand, London WC2N 5JE, England
Distributed in Australia by Capricorn Link Ltd.
P.O. Box 665, Lane Cove, NSW 2066
Manufactured in the United States of America
Printed and bound in Hong Kong
All rights reserved

Sterling ISBN 0-8069-0849-1

Contents

Preface

Overwhelmed by a thousand burdens, I generally refuse most firmly to write a preface for a book, no matter how dear a friend or respected an author is involved.

So why did I ask, solicit, demand to write this particular preface?

Marta Pulini, Francesco Antonucci, and Gianni Salvaterra live and work in New York, a city with which I am madly in love, but their book has the flavor of memories—for them, for me.

The dishes described in this book were present all during my childhood as well as my adult years. Just as they continue to delight me today, they will no doubt do so in the future. Some of these dishes are Parmesan-Cheese Ice Cream, Pears, Aceto Balsamico Tradizionale di Modena; Polenta Fettuccine, Cotechino Sausage, Cannellini Beans; Eel, Butternut Squash, Pumpkin Seeds; Salt Cod, Chickpeas, Rosemary; and Semifreddo with Torrone Nougat, Oranges.

In this book I have found the dishes of our past, as described by Marta, a cook who has definitely mastered her art, and Francesco, a gastronome and owner of his own restaurant in New York, called Remi, which is known far and wide, and illustrated by Gianni, a photographer who delights in challenging assignments. And it is precisely because of their testimony that these dishes will become the dishes of today and tomorrow. They are the kind of dishes that have established all over the world the superiority of the Italian way of cooking, and they will continue to do so with their immediate appeal and their pleasant and imaginative combination of healthy ingredients.

Gastronomy advances right along with civilization. It is considered a trivial art only by trivial people, who think that it is intended to satisfy appetites. That is the purpose of eating, not of gastronomy.

For anyone who wants to become immersed in the history and geography of a people, gastronomy is a sure and fascinating road.

One cannot help but be proud that every one of the dishes described here underlines the categorical imperative of *clean* foods, in the same way that people demand *clean* oceans, mountains, lakes, rivers, hills, fields, and woods. These dishes are all very different, but each one is the result of a thousand years of gestures that have been repeated over and over again to meet the needs of ordinary people who appreciate good food.

I would like to quote the following passage by Afra Bianchin Scarpa, a most excellent designer and a partner of the Seminario Permanente (Luigi Veronelli Institute) that also bears my name: "It strikes us as a paradox that the enjoyment of good eating and drinking, which appears to be such a short-lived experience (perhaps this is why the art of making good food and drink, just like that of design, has in the past been considered a servile art), is the first necessary step and the first teaching tool for the development of individual taste. Although it is true that the whole process runs its course within the time of the actual experience, i.e. with the physical phenomenon, it is also true that the knowledge we have obtained, the secrets we have discovered, and the mysteries of which we have become aware are transformed into memories that remain vivid."

For me, this book is indeed the recovery of memories, because my roots are here and, I admit, also my vocation—gastronomy.

Luigi Veronelli

Introduction

Can the images that are constantly repeated and at the same time constantly renewed, as well as the reassuring names and the precise gestures, remain meaningful to us personally in the kitchen?

We have tried to present our affirmative answer in this book.

In choosing the names of the recipes, we have carefully avoided giving any indications about the type of cooking called for in each one. This was done so that your attention would not be diverted from the fundamental importance of the ingredients. They always remain true to themselves and to those essential qualities that distinguish them from each other.

For this book, we have chosen one basic ingredient that is typical of each region of Italy and combined it in each recipe with other ingredients in accordance with the traditional canons of good taste. In so doing, we have tried to identify and, to some extent, also invent a theme that is common to all four courses of each meal. We hope that the invited guests will experience our meals like "musical symphonies of taste" that will bring them blissful satisfaction.

Gianni Salvaterra

VALLE D'AOSTA

Juniper

DEER, RED BEETS, JUNIPER

▼

Preparation Time: 1 hour, plus 6 hours for marinating

Ingredients for 6 Servings

For the Deer:

1 lb. boneless loin of deer

3 cups dry red wine

2 celery stalks

2 carrots

1 onion

10 juniper berries

3 bay leaves

Black pepper

¼ cup extra virgin olive oil

For the Garnish:

4 medium-sized beets

2 tablespoons extra virgin olive oil

For the Sauce:

6 juniper berries

Salt

White pepper

1 lemon

3 tablespoons extra virgin olive oil

1 tablespoon gin

Preparation

The Deer: After removing the fatty and fibrous parts from the loin of deer, place it in a saucepan and add enough red wine to cover the meat. Add the vegetables, cut in slices, as well as the juniper, bay leaves, and a dash of ground black pepper. Let marinate in the refrigerator for 6 hours. Remove the loin from the marinade, drain, and dry with a cloth. Brown on all sides in olive oil over high heat in a heavy pan, leaving it rare on the inside. Let it rest in a cool place.

The Garnish: Cook the red beets in plenty of salted water until they are done. Drain and let them cool.

The Sauce: Crush the juniper berries in a bowl. Add a dash of salt, a dash of white pepper, and the juice of the lemon. Beat with a whisk until the salt is dissolved. Blend in the olive oil and the gin, stirring constantly until the sauce is thoroughly emulsified.

To Serve: Peel the red beets and cut them into very thin slices. Toss them with extra virgin olive oil. Arrange the slices in a circle on a platter. Cut the meat into paper-thin slices and place these on top. Pour the spicy sauce over the meat.

POTATO GNOCCHI, VENISON, JUNIPER

Preparation Time: 3 hours

Ingredients for 6 Servings

For the Ragout:
1 carrot
1 onion
1 celery stalk
Extra virgin olive oil
1 lb. boneless venison
shoulder (trimmed)
8 juniper berries, crushed
1 cup dry red wine
7 oz. peeled tomatoes
1 bouquet garni (see Basic
Recipes)
Salt and pepper
Vegetable stock (see Basic
Recipes)

For the Potato Gnocchi:
5 medium-sized potatoes
2¼ cups flour
2 oz. Parmesan cheese, grated
4 eggs
Nutmeg
Salt and pepper

Preparation

The Ragout: Cut the vegetables into very small cubes and brown in extra virgin olive oil. Cut the meat into very small cubes and brown with the vegetables. Add the crushed juniper berries and red wine, cooking over high heat until the wine has evaporated. Add the tomatoes, bouquet garni, and salt and pepper, and let the mixture cook for about 1 hour. (If the sauce dries up, add a little water or vegetable stock.)

The Potato Gnocchi: Cook the potatoes in their skins for about 30 minutes in a large quantity of salted water, until they are tender to the touch when pricked with a fork. Remove from the water and peel with a knife while they are still hot, using a cloth to hold them. Mash at once in a potato masher over a clean work surface, cover with a cloth, and let cool for about half an hour. Add the remaining ingredients to the cooled potatoes, and blend with your hands for a few minutes until the consistency of the mixture is uniform. Sprinkle additional flour on the work surface, divide the dough into pieces, and shape them into 1-inch rolls. Cut them with a spatula into small ½-inch sections. Place a pan with slightly salted water on the stove and bring to a boil. Add the gnocchi and cook until they float to the top. Remove them with a slotted spoon.

To Serve: Remove the bouquet garni, and serve the hot ragout on individual plates. Place the steaming gnocchi on top.

Duck, Cabbage, Enfer d'Arvier Wine, Juniper

Preparation Time: 2 hours

Ingredients for 4 Servings

For the Sauce:
1 shallot
¼ cup butter
2 cups Enfer d'Arvier (dry red wine from Valle d'Aosta)
10 juniper berries
2 cups duck stock (see Basic Recipes)
Salt

For the Duck:
2 medium-sized domestic ducks, cleaned
Salt
4 bay leaves
2 tablespoons extra virgin olive oil
1 medium-sized cabbage, cleaned with the tough outer leaves removed
4 tablespoons red wine vinegar
Vegetable stock (see Basic Recipes)
Pepper

Preparation

The Sauce: Chop the shallot, place in a saucepan, and brown in the butter. Add the red wine and whole juniper berries, and cook until the sauce is reduced by half. Add the duck stock, and let thicken for a few more minutes. Strain through a fine-mesh colander, add salt to taste, and keep in a warm place.

The Duck: Wash the ducks and pat them dry; sprinkle with salt and insert the bay leaves. Place them in a saucepan greased with the olive oil, and let them brown over high heat. Add the cabbage leaves and the red wine vinegar. Sprinkle with pepper. Preheat the oven to 375° to 400°F, and cook for about 1 hour, basting from time to time with the vegetable stock so that they do not dry out.

To Serve: Place the hot cabbage leaves on individual plates. Carve the duck and place on top of the cabbage; top with the sauce.

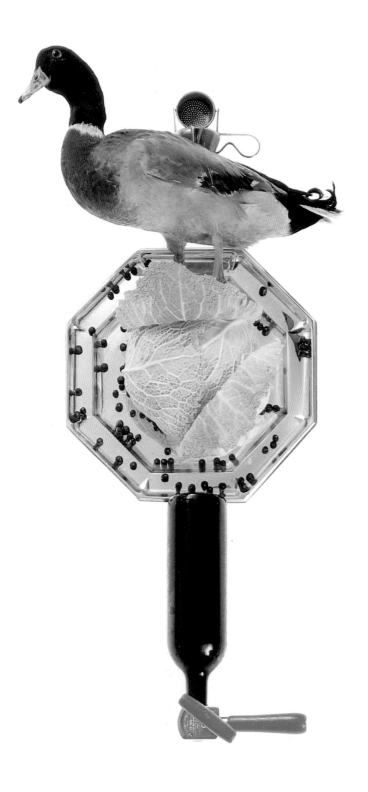

PEARS, MOSCATO DI CHAMBAVE WINE, JUNIPER, HAZELNUTS

Preparation Time: 1 hour

Ingredients for 4 Servings

For the Pears:
4 pears
Half a bottle of Moscato di Chambave
(a dessert white wine from Valle d'Aosta)
2 tablespoons sugar
10 juniper berries
¾ cup shelled hazelnuts

Preparation

The Pears: Peel the pears, but do not remove the stems. Place them in a deep pan just large enough to hold them. Add the wine, sugar, whole juniper berries, and enough water to cover the pears up to the stems. Bake at 300°F with an aluminum foil cover until the pears are tender but not too well done. Remove them carefully, place on a plate, and let the liquid in which they were cooked boil down until it has the consistency of syrup. Toast the hazelnuts in a preheated 350°F oven for about 10 minutes. Let them cool and then chop coarsely.

To Serve: Place the pears on plates, top with the sauce, and sprinkle with the chopped hazelnuts. (You may finish off the plates by adding a heaping spoonful of hazelnut ice cream.)

LOMBARDY

Rice

RICE, ARTICHOKES, SAFFRON

▼

Preparation Time: 2 hours

Ingredients for 6 Servings

For the Saffron Risotto:
Half an onion
4 tablespoons extra virgin olive oil
1½ cups rice (Carnaroli, Vialone Nano, or Arborio)
½ cup dry white wine
Vegetable stock
¾ cup butter
½ cup Parmesan cheese, grated
½ teaspoon saffron threads
Salt and pepper

For the Artichokes:
18 baby artichokes
2 cloves garlic, crushed
4 tablespoons extra virgin olive oil
Salt and pepper

½ cup Parmesan cheese, grated

Preparation

The Saffron Risotto: Prepare a risotto (see Basic Recipes), and add the saffron threads just before the risotto is done.

The Risotto Pancakes: Melt a pat of butter in a nonstick skillet until the butter sizzles. Place two heaping spoonfuls of the saffron risotto in the skillet, spreading it out evenly, and cook until the risotto reaches a golden-brown color. Use a lid of the same size to help in turning over the risotto pancake, and brown it on the other side for two more minutes. When it is done, place the pancake on a paper towel to remove any excess grease. Continue making risotto pancakes until all the rice is used up.

The Artichokes: Remove the tough outer leaves, cut in half, then slice. Sauté in the olive oil together with the garlic. Add salt and pepper.

To Serve: Place the artichokes on top of the risotto pancakes, sprinkle with grated Parmesan cheese, and dot with butter. Place in a preheated broiler until a crisp, golden crust forms. Serve hot on individual plates.

RICE, GORGONZOLA, WALNUTS, SPINACH

▼

Preparation Time: 40 minutes

Ingredients for 6 Servings

For the Garnish:
6 walnuts, shelled

For the Risotto:
1 onion
4 tablespoons extra virgin olive oil
3 cups rice (Carnaroli, Vialone Nano, or Arborio)
1 cup dry white wine
Vegetable stock
2 cups small spinach leaves (without the stems)
5½ oz. Gorgonzola cheese
Salt and pepper

Preparation

The Garnish: Coarsely chop the walnuts and set them aside.

The Risotto: Wash and dry the spinach leaves very carefully. Prepare a risotto (see Basic Recipes), and add the spinach and half the Gorgonzola about halfway through the cooking time. Finish cooking the risotto and remove from the stove. Whip in the remaining Gorgonzola and add salt and pepper to taste. (Note: Make sure that the Gorgonzola is at room temperature.)

To Serve: Sprinkle the risotto with the chopped walnuts, and serve on heated plates. (Note that neither butter nor Parmesan cheese is used in this risotto recipe because of the creaminess and flavor of the Gorgonzola.)

OSSOBUCO, STRAVECCHIO BRANDY, RICE, LEMON

▼

Preparation Time: 3 hours

Ingredients for 6 Servings

For the Ossobuco:
6 veal shanks, 10 to
11 oz. each
⅓ cup flour
Extra virgin olive oil
1 stalk celery
1 carrot
1 onion
¼ cup butter
2 cups Stravecchio brandy
1½ qts. veal stock
(see Basic Recipes)
1 bouquet garni
(see Basic Recipes)
Vegetable stock
(see Basic Recipes)
Salt and pepper

For the Lemon Risotto:
Half an onion
4 tablespoons extra virgin
olive oil
2 cups rice (Carnaroli,
Vialone Nano, or Arborio)
½ cup dry white wine
Vegetable stock
½ cup butter
2 tablespoons Parmesan
cheese, grated
1 lemon

Preparation

The Ossobuco: Flour the veal shanks, place them in a nonstick skillet, and brown them in olive oil until they are golden. Chop the vegetables, brown in oil and butter, and add to the veal shanks. Pour the Stravecchio over the meat and heat until evaporated. Add the veal stock and bouquet garni. Cover and let the shanks cook for about two hours in a preheated 300°F oven. Make sure the sauce covers the meat at all times (add some vegetable stock if necessary). Remove the veal shanks from the skillet and set in a warm place. Heat the sauce until it is reduced by half, and add salt and pepper to taste. Keep warm.

The Lemon Risotto: Grate the rind of the lemon, but make sure not to use the white part, which has a bitter taste. Prepare a risotto (see Basic Recipes), and add the grated lemon rind just before the risotto is done.

To Serve: Top the veal shanks with a little sauce, and serve on individual plates with the lemon risotto.

Rice, Vanilla, Pistachios, Apricots

▼

Preparation time: 90 minutes

Ingredients for 4 Servings

For the Apricots:
4 medium-sized apricots, not too ripe
¾ cup sugar
1 vanilla bean
1 stick cinnamon

For the Rice Pudding:
¾ cup rice (Carnaroli, Vialone Nano, or Arborio)
½ qt. milk
½ qt. heavy cream
1 vanilla bean
1 small cinnamon stick
½ cup sugar
5⅓ oz. Mascarpone cheese
⅓ to ½ cup shelled pistachios

Preparation

The Apricots: Wash the apricots and cut in half; remove the pits. Set aside. Combine half a quart of water and the sugar in a saucepan; heat and stir until the sugar dissolves. Add the vanilla bean (cut open lengthwise) and cinnamon stick, and bring to a boil. Now add the apricots, remove the pan from the burner, and leave them to cool in the syrup.

The Rice Pudding: Place the rice in a pan and add the milk, cream, vanilla bean (after making a lengthwise incision with a knife), and cinnamon stick. Place the pan over moderate heat and bring to a boil. Let the mixture cook, stirring frequently until the rice is tender. When done, remove from the burner and discard the vanilla bean and cinnamon stick. Add the sugar and mix well. Let cool and add the Mascarpone, blending it in carefully. Toast and finely chop the pistachios. Mix them into the rice.

To Serve: Place the rice pudding in individual dessert bowls, and garnish with the apricots.

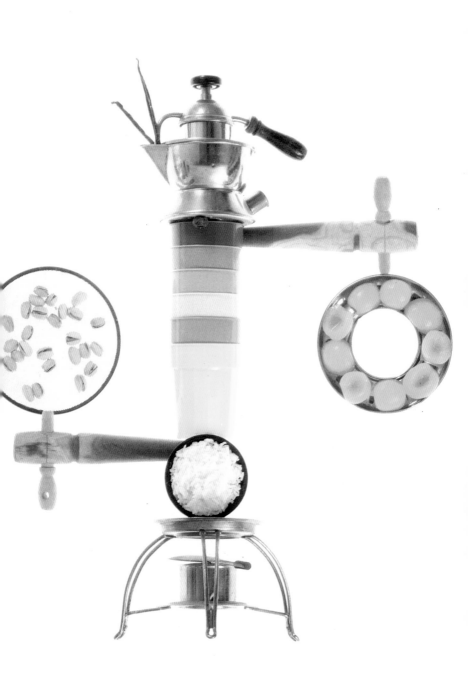

LIGURIA

Basil

RED MULLET, BLACK OLIVES, BASIL, VEGETABLES

▼

Preparation Time: 1 hour

Ingredients for 4 Servings

For the Fried Vegetables:
1 red beet
½ celery root
1 carrot
3 baby artichokes
1 cup corn oil
Salt

For the Red Mullet:
2 tablespoons extra virgin olive oil (preferably from Liguria)
4 red mullets, about 7 oz. each, cleaned
⅓ cup flour
32 pitted black olives
1 cup dry white wine
20 basil leaves
¼ cup butter
Salt and pepper

Preparation

The Fried Vegetables: Cut the vegetables in very thin strips with a mandoline or a knife. Fry them in plenty of hot vegetable oil until they are crisp. Then transfer them to paper towels to absorb the excess oil. Add salt to taste, and set aside in a warm place.

The Red Mullets: Pour the olive oil in an oven-proof heavy-bottomed skillet. Dust the mullets with flour, and brown them on each side in the skillet over low heat for about 2 minutes. Add the black olives and white wine. Place the skillet in a preheated 350°F oven for about 10 minutes. Remove the mullets from the skillet when they are cooked through and fillet them. Place on a tray and set aside in a warm place. Chop the basil leaves, and blend them into the sauce together with the butter. Add salt and pepper to taste.

To Serve: Place a mullet in the middle of each plate. Top with a little sauce and garnish with the fried vegetables.

Sole, Basil, and Pine-Nut Tortelli

▼

Preparation Time: 2 hours

Ingredients for 6 Servings

For the Filling:
2 medium-sized Idaho potatoes
4 fillets of sole about 3 oz. each
4 tablespoons extra virgin olive oil (preferably from Liguria)
Salt and pepper
1 clove garlic, finely chopped
10 basil leaves
1 tablespoon chopped parsley

For the Tortelli Dough:
3¾ cups flour
5 eggs
Salt

For the Sole Tortelli Seasoning:
½ cup of fish stock (see Basic Recipes)
2 tablespoons butter

For the Pesto Sauce:
6 basil leaves
1 bunch of parsley
1 teaspoon pine nuts
1 teaspoon aged Pecorino cheese
1 teaspoon grated Parmesan cheese
6 tablespoons extra virgin olive oil, preferably from Liguria
½ clove garlic
Salt

Preparation

The Stuffing: Slice the potatoes very thin and blanch for 5 minutes in salted boiling water. Place them together with the fillets of sole on a nonstick sheet greased with some of the oil. Sprinkle with salt and pepper, the finely chopped garlic, herbs, and remaining oil. Cover with aluminum foil and place in a preheated 375° to 400°F oven for about 10 minutes or until the ingredients are cooked and the liquid is absorbed. When fully cooked, let cool and chop very fine.

The Pesto Sauce: Place all the ingredients in a food processor with 2 tablespoons of extra virgin olive oil and blend until smooth. Remove the mixture and add the remaining oil. Mix well.

The Sole Tortelli: Roll out a thin sheet of dough and prepare the tortelli (see Basic Recipes). Cook them in plenty of salted water and drain carefully. Meanwhile, combine the fish stock in a nonstick skillet with the butter, and heat until reduced by half.

To Serve: Sauté the sole tortelli in the same skillet. Place on warm plates, topping with the pesto sauce at room temperature.

TUNA, BLACK PEPPER, BASIL OLIVE OIL, CHILI PEPPER

▼

Preparation Time: 30 minutes, plus 2 hours for cooling

Ingredients for 6 Servings

For the Tuna:
1½ to 2 lbs. fillet of fresh tuna
2 tablespoons ground black pepper
Salt

For the Basil Olive Oil:
50 basil leaves
1 clove garlic
1 chili pepper
10 tablespoons extra virgin olive oil
(preferably from Liguria)
1 lemon

Preparation

The Tuna: Clean the tuna fillet, removing the skin and dark parts. Try to give the fillet a cylindrical shape. Sprinkle the black pepper on aluminum foil, and roll the tuna fillet tightly in it, making sure that you cover the entire surface evenly. Place the tuna fillet, wrapped in the aluminum foil, in a skillet and sear at moderate heat for about 1 minute, turning it on all sides. Remove it from the skillet, and let it cool in the refrigerator for about two hours, still wrapped in the aluminum foil.

The Basil Olive Oil: Blanch the basil leaves and dry them carefully with a cloth. Process them in a blender together with the garlic and the top part of the chili pepper. Add the extra virgin olive oil a little at a time until the mixture is smooth and resembles a light pesto sauce.

To Serve: Remove the tuna fillet from the aluminum foil, and cut in very thin slices. Place the slices on plates, adding a little salt and topping with a tablespoon of sauce. Squeeze a few drops of lemon juice on each.

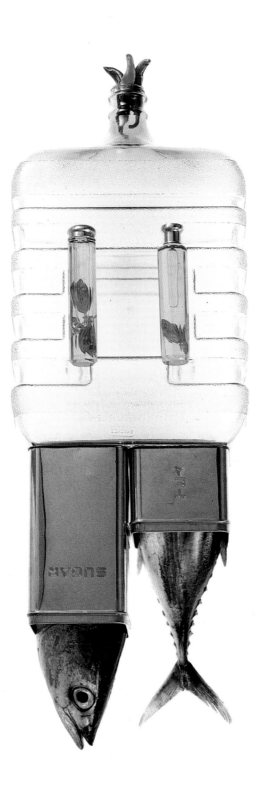

BASIL SORBET

▼

Preparation Time: 30 minutes, plus 15 minutes in an ice-cream machine (or 5 hours in the freezer)

Ingredients for 4 Servings

For the Basil Sorbet:
3¼ cups sugar
40 basil leaves
1 lime

For the Garnish:
4 small basil leaves

Preparation

The Basil Sorbet: Dissolve the sugar in ½ quart of water in a saucepan over moderate heat. Boil another 5 minutes to reduce it some more. Turn off the heat, and add the basil leaves and the juice of the lime. Let the mixture rest until it cools off. Strain the mixture through a fine-mesh sieve, and pour it into an ice-cream machine. (If you don't have an ice-cream machine, pour the mixture into a very large bowl and put it in the freezer, stirring frequently until it reaches the right consistency.)

To Serve: Serve the sorbet in individual bowls, decorating each with a basil leaf.

PIEDMONT

Dolcetto Wine

CROSTINI, MARROW, WHITE TRUFFLES, DOLCETTO WINE

▼

Preparation Time: 45 minutes

Ingredients for 6 Servings

For the Sauce:
½ shallot

2 tablespoons extra virgin olive oil

2 cups Dolcetto wine (a dry red wine from Piedmont, can be substituted for with an American Pinot Noir)

⅓ cup butter

For the Crostini:
1 small loaf French bread

1 lb. beef marrow cut in 1-inch pieces

Salt and pepper

2 oz. white truffles (preferably from Alba)

Preparation

The Sauce: Brown the shallot in the olive oil in a nonstick skillet. Add the wine and cook until reduced by half. Remove from the burner, blend in the butter, and stir until the sauce thickens.

The Crostini: Slice the bread ⅜ inch thick, and toast lightly. Check the marrow for any possible bone shards, and brown for a few seconds in a nonstick skillet without adding any oil or butter. Place the marrow on the crostini, add salt and pepper to taste, and place in a preheated 375° to 400°F oven for a few minutes until the marrow becomes golden brown.

To Serve: Serve the crostini while still hot, topped with the marrow and some of the red wine sauce, and sprinkled with very thinly sliced chips of white truffle.

GREEN PAPPARDELLE, PHEASANT, DOLCETTO WINE

▼

Preparation Time: 2 hours

Ingredients for 6 Servings

For the Meat Sauce:

1 medium-sized pheasant hen, cleaned
1 carrot
1 onion
1 celery stalk
4 tablespoons extra virgin olive oil
¼ cup butter
2 cloves garlic, pressed
1 cup Dolcetto wine (a dry red wine from Piedmont, can be substituted for with an American Pinot Noir)
5 oz. peeled tomatoes
1 bouquet garni (see Basic Recipes)
Salt and pepper

For the Green Pappardelle Dough:

2 cups spinach leaves
4½ cups flour
4 eggs
Salt

Preparation

The Meat Sauce: Wash the pheasant well in running water, pat it dry, and cut it into four parts. Chop the vegetables. Heat the oil and butter in a heavy-bottomed skillet until they sizzle. Add the pheasant and garlic cloves, and brown over high heat. Add the vegetables and Dolcetto wine, and cook until the wine has evaporated. Then add the peeled tomatoes and bouquet garni. Cover and cook over moderate heat for about 1 hour. When done, remove the pheasant and bone it. Shred the meat and place it back in the sauce. Add salt and pepper to taste. Keep in a warm place.

The Green Pappardelle: Clean, wash, blanch, and drain the spinach leaves, and carefully squeeze them dry with a kitchen towel. Chop them in a food processor. Prepare the pasta dough (see Basic Recipes), and add the spinach in the beginning, together with the eggs. Roll the dough out to a thin sheet on a smooth, clean surface. After it has dried slightly, shape it into pappardelle (see Basic Recipes). Cook in plenty of boiling salted water, and drain when it is still slightly underdone.

To Serve: Sauté the green pappardelle with the meat sauce in a nonstick skillet, mix well, and serve on hot plates.

PIKE, SHALLOT, DOLCETTO WINE

▼

Preparation Time: 1 hour

Ingredients for 4 Servings

For the Sauce:
*1 bottle Dolcetto wine (a dry red wine from Piedmont, can be
substituted for with an American Pinot Noir)*
6 cloves
Salt

For the Pike:
3 shallots
4 pike fillets, about 8 oz. each
3 tablespoons extra virgin olive oil
8 bay leaves
¼ cup butter

Preparation

The Sauce: Heat the red wine and the cloves in a saucepan.
Let boil until reduced by half. Add salt to taste, and keep in
a warm place.

The Pike: Slice the shallots and brown in a saucepan with the
olive oil and bay leaves. Place the pike fillet in a buttered oven-
proof pan, and spread the sautéed shallots over them. Place
in a preheated 475°F oven, and cook for about 15 minutes.
Remove the pike fillets from the pan, add the wine sauce, and
cook for another 10 minutes to reduce the sauce. Remove the
cloves.

To Serve: Place the pike fillets on warm plates, and top with
the sauce.

BERRIES, PEACHES, YOGURT, DOLCETTO WINE

Preparation Time: 1 hour

Ingredients for 4 Servings

For the Fruit Soup:
½ cup raspberries
½ cup blackberries
½ cup red currants
4 medium-sized peaches, not too ripe
1 orange
1 vanilla bean
2 cups Dolcetto wine (a dry red wine from Piedmont, can be substituted for with an American Pinot Noir)
3 tablespoons sugar

For the Garnish:
7 oz. yogurt
2 tablespoons sugar
½ teaspoon ground cinnamon

Preparation

The Fruit Soup: Clean and wash the berries, leaving them whole. Peel the peaches, remove the pits, and cut them in wedges. Cut the rind of the orange into fine julienne (make sure not to use the white part, which has a bitter taste). Combine in a saucepan the fruit, wine, sugar, and vanilla bean, cut open lengthwise. Cook about 20 minutes over moderate heat, stirring carefully. Remove from the heat and let cool.

The Garnish: Combine the sugar and the cinnamon with the yogurt in a bowl and mix well.

To Serve: Serve the fruit soup in individual dessert bowls, and top with a heaping tablespoon of flavored yogurt.

TRENTINO

Apple

SPECK, APPLES, LIVER OF VENISON

▼

Preparation Time: 1 hour

Ingredients for 4 Servings

For the Vinaigrette Sauce:
6 or 7 shallots
½ cup of veal stock (see Basic Recipes)
8 tablespoons extra virgin olive oil
3 tablespoons raspberry vinegar
Salt and pepper

For the Venison Liver:
1 whole liver of venison, about 14 oz.
Salt and pepper
Caul fat (enough to wrap the liver)
¼ cup butter

For the Garnish:
3½ oz. mâche
7 oz. piece of speck (smoke-cured prosciutto from Trentino)
¼ cup butter
2 green apples

Preparation

The Vinaigrette Sauce: Peel and chop the shallots; then heat them in a skillet together with the veal stock. Add the olive oil and the raspberry vinegar. Season with salt and pepper. Keep warm.

The Venison Liver: Soften the liver in lukewarm water. Pat it dry and remove the skin very carefully, trying not to pierce the tissue. Season with salt and pepper, and wrap it in the caul fat. Place in a saucepan of just the right size and add the butter. Cook it in a preheated 350°F oven for about 20 minutes or until it is done on the outside but still pink inside. Remove from the oven, discard what is left of the caul, and keep the liver in a warm place.

The Garnish: Wash and dry the mâche. Finely dice the speck, and brown it in 2 tablespoons of the butter. Peel the apples and cut them into thin wedges. Sauté the apples with the remaining butter until golden brown on both sides.

To Serve: Place the mâche and the speck on plates. Cut the liver into slices (not too thin!), and place on top. Sprinkle with the vinaigrette sauce. Garnish with the apple wedges.

Whole-Wheat Tagliatelle, Green Apples, Walnuts, Poppy Seeds

Preparation Time: 90 minutes

Ingredients for 4 Servings

For the Sauce:
4 green apples
1 lemon
24 walnuts (4 of which are for the garnish)
½ cup butter
2 teaspoons poppy seeds
Nutmeg
Salt and pepper

For the Whole-Wheat Tagliatelle Dough:
1½ cups flour
1½ cups whole-wheat flour
4 eggs
Salt

Preparation

The Sauce: Peel the apples, cut them in slices, and marinate in a bowl with the lemon juice for about 15 minutes. Crack the walnuts; take 20 and chop them up coarsely, keeping 4 as whole kernels. Brown the apples in a skillet with half of the butter; then add the chopped nuts, the poppy seeds, and a little ground nutmeg. Add salt and pepper to taste. Remove from the burner and keep warm.

The Whole-Wheat Tagliatelle: Roll out a thin sheet of pasta dough (see Basic Recipes) on a clean, smooth surface. Let it dry slightly, and prepare the tagliatelle (see Basic Recipes). Cook them in plenty of boiling salted water. Drain just before they are completely done, and reserve some of the cooking water.

To Serve: Sauté the whole-wheat tagliatelle with the sauce in a nonstick skillet. If the pasta gets too dry, add the rest of the butter and a little of the reserved water. Add salt and pepper if necessary. Serve on individual plates decorated with the whole walnut kernels.

PORK, APPLES, HORSERADISH, CINNAMON

▼

Preparation Time: 2 hours

Ingredients for 4 Servings

For the Apple Sauce:
6 ripe apples
1 teaspoon cinnamon
½ teaspoon freshly grated horseradish
4 teaspoons sugar

For the Smoked Pork Shank:
2 smoked pork shanks of medium size
2 carrots
1 celery stalk
1 onion
1 cup corn oil
Salt and pepper
2 cups dry white wine
1 quart of vegetable stock (see Basic Recipes)
⅓ cup butter
1 bouquet garni (see Basic Recipes)

Preparation

The Apple Sauce: Peel and core the apples, cut them up coarsely, and cook in very little water for about 10 minutes. Place in a blender with the cinnamon, horseradish, and sugar, and process until the mixture becomes a rather thick sauce. Cover and keep in a warm place.

The Smoked Pork Shank: Clean and trim the shanks. Cut the vegetables into small chunks. Brown the shanks with the corn oil in an oven-proof roasting pan big enough to hold them. Sprinkle with salt and pepper; add the vegetables and 1 cup of the dry white wine. Continue to cook them in a preheated 375° to 400°F oven for about 1 hour, making sure to turn every 10 minutes. Baste with some of the vegetable stock from time to time. If the meat should brown too quickly on top, cover it with aluminum foil. When the shanks are done, remove them from the oven and keep warm. Remove the grease from the cooking juices, and mix in the rest of the white wine. Add the remaining vegetable stock, and reduce the liquid by half. Thicken with the butter, add salt to taste, and put through a fine-mesh strainer.

To Serve: Carefully remove the meat from the bones, and place on individual heated plates. Top with the cooking juices, and add a heaping spoonful of the apple sauce.

APPLES, ALMONDS, AMARETTI COOKIES

▼

Preparation Time: 1 hour

Ingredients for 4 Servings

For the Filling:
2 green apples
8 amaretti cookies (macaroons)
⅓ cup almonds
6 tablespoons heavy cream
2 teaspoons white sugar
Rind of 1 lemon, grated
Salt

For the Apples:
4 Golden Delicious apples

For the Garnish:
1 teaspoon cinnamon

Preparation

The Filling: Peel and grate the green apples. Chop up the amaretti cookies and the almonds. Place all the ingredients in a bowl, and mix until well blended.

The Apples au Gratin: Cut the Golden Delicious apples in half lengthwise and core them. Fill the middle of each half with the filling. Place the apples in a baking pan lined with wax paper. Preheat the oven to 350°F and bake them until they are soft and the gratin is browned (for about 30 minutes).

To Serve: Serve the hot apples au gratin on individual plates. Sprinkle with a dash of cinnamon.

VENETO

Corn

POLENTA, DUCK LIVERS

▼

Preparation Time: 2 hours

Ingredients for 6 Servings

For the Fried Polenta:
2 cups cornmeal for polenta (fine-grained)
2 teaspoons olive oil
Salt
¼ cup butter

For the Sauce:
1 cup duck stock (see Basic Recipes)
¼ cup white grappa
Salt and pepper

For the Duck-Liver Sausage
15 duck livers
Salt and pepper
1 hog casing
1 shallot
½ cup butter
3 sprigs of thyme
4 bay leaves

Preparation

The Fried Polenta: Prepare a rather firm polenta (see Basic Recipes). When done, place it on a sheet pan and let cool. Cut it in irregular rectangles (about 2 × 3 inches), and brown in the butter on both sides. Keep warm.

The Duck-Liver Sausage: Soften the duck livers in lukewarm water. Let them drain and pat dry. Carefully remove all traces of bile and the veins. Finely slice the livers, and sprinkle them with salt and pepper. Fit them into the pork casing, shaping it like a sausage. Close the casing. Brown the chopped shallot with butter in an oven-proof skillet. Add the thyme and bay leaves, and brown the sausage for a few minutes. Place in a preheated 425°F oven, and cook until the sausage is brown on the outside but still pink inside.

The Sauce: Remove the grease from the cooking juices of the duck livers; then add the grappa and duck stock, and cook over moderate heat until reduced by half. Add salt and pepper to taste, and put through a fine-mesh strainer.

To Serve: Arrange a few slices of polenta on the warm plates. Cut the duck-liver sausage into ⅜-inch slices, and place on top of the polenta. Pour the sauce over them.

Polenta Fettuccine, Cotechino Sausage, Cannellini Beans

▼

Preparation Time: 3 hours, plus 6 hours for soaking the beans

Ingredients for 8 Servings

For the Meat Sauce:
1 cup cannellini beans

½ onion

1 celery stalk

1 carrot

1 cotechino pork sausage, of about 1 lb.

¼ cup butter

2 sprigs rosemary

⅓ cup tomato sauce (see Basic Recipes)

Salt and pepper

1 cup Parmesan cheese, grated

For the Polenta Fettuccine Dough:
2 teaspoons extra virgin olive oil

1⅓ cups cornmeal for polenta (fine-grained)

Salt

1½ cups white flour

5 eggs

Preparation

The Meat Sauce: Soak the dried beans in lukewarm water for about 6 hours. Drain them, place in a pot filled with lightly salted water, and add the vegetables cut in small chunks. Place on the burner, and cook until the beans are tender. Drain them and set aside. Prick the cotechino all around, and place it in a pot filled with cold water. Bring the water to a boil, and simmer the sausage over moderate heat for about 45 minutes. When done, remove it from the liquid, discard the skin, and use a fork to crumble it coarsely. Keep in a warm place. Brown the butter and rosemary in a nonstick skillet, and add the beans, crumbled sausage, and tomato sauce. Cook for a few minutes, mixing the ingredients well. Add salt and pepper to taste.

The Polenta Fettuccine: Prepare a soft polenta (see Basic Recipes); then turn it out on a clean surface. When the temperature of the polenta allows you to work it with your hands, add all the other ingredients. Mix them well and prepare a pasta dough (see Basic Recipes). Roll it out to a thin sheet on a clean surface, and shape the fettuccine (see Basic Recipes). Cook them in plenty of boiling salted water, and drain carefully while they are still slightly underdone.

To Serve: Sauté the polenta fettuccine in a nonstick skillet together with the meat sauce, mixing in the grated Parmesan cheese. Serve nice and hot on individual plates.

POLENTA, FROGS' LEGS, PARSLEY

Preparation Time: 2 hours

Ingredients for 6 Servings

For the Polenta:
2 cups cornmeal for polenta (fine-grained)
2 teaspoons extra virgin olive oil
Salt

For the Batter:
4 eggs
¾ cup flour
½ cup lager beer
Salt

For the Frogs' Legs:
24 frogs' legs
½ cup red wine vinegar
1 quart corn oil

For the Garnish:
2 medium bunches of parsley

Preparation

The Polenta: Prepare a soft polenta (see Basic Recipes), remove from the heat, and keep warm.

The Batter: Combine the egg yolks with the flour in a bowl. Mix well and add the beer. Beat the egg whites until stiff, and fold into the mixture. (If the mixture is too thick, add a little water.) Add salt to taste.

The Frogs' Legs: Wash the frogs' legs with cold water and vinegar and pat dry. Heat the corn oil in a large frying pan. Dip the frogs' legs in the batter, and fry for about 2 minutes on both sides until they are golden brown. Drain and dry on paper towels. Fry the parsley in the same oil; drain and dry.

To Serve: Serve the polenta nice and hot on individual plates, and place the fried frogs' legs on top. Sprinkle with fried parsley.

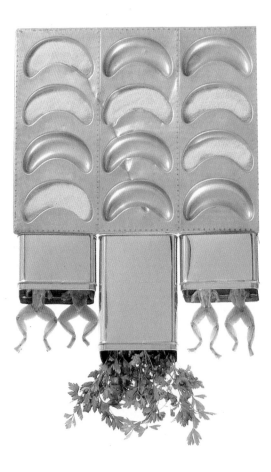

POLENTA, GRAPPA, PEARS

▼

Preparation Time: 75 minutes

Ingredients for 6 Servings

For the Polenta Cakes:
1 cup butter
1 cup sugar
9 eggs
1 cup cornmeal for polenta (fine-grained)
1½ cups almond flour
½ cup potato starch

For the Pear Sauce:
4 medium-sized ripe pears
1⅓ tablespoons sugar
1 tablespoon potato starch
1 vanilla bean
2 tablespoons pear grappa

Preparation

The Polenta Cakes: Whip the butter with the sugar in a mixing bowl. Add 5 egg yolks and the remaining 4 whole eggs. Mix well with a whisk. Add the cornmeal, the almond flour, and the starch, a little at a time, while continuing to beat briskly with the whisk. Butter 3-inch moulds with sides about 1½ inches high, and pour in the mixture. Preheat the oven to 350°F, and bake for about 30 minutes. Remove from the oven, and turn them over when they reach room temperature.

The Pear Sauce: Peel the pears, discard the seeds, and process in a blender with the sugar and the potato starch. Place the mixture in a saucepan, and add the vanilla bean, cut open lengthwise. Cook over low heat, stirring with a wooden spoon, until the mixture starts to boil. Remove from the heat, discard the vanilla bean, and add the pear grappa.

The Serve: Pour the pear sauce over the plates, and place the polenta cake on top.

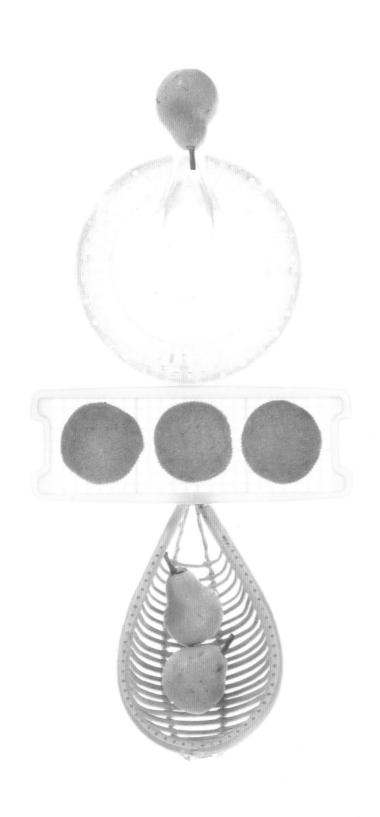

FRIULI

Squash

SHRIMP, BUTTERNUT SQUASH, ZUCCHINI, ZUCCHINI BLOSSOMS

▼

Preparation Time: 1 hour

Ingredients for 4 Servings

For the Shrimp Batter:
3 eggs
1½ cups flour
⅔ cup lager beer
Salt

For the Vegetable Batter:
3 eggs
1½ cups flour
½ cup milk
Salt

For the Fry:
16 shrimp
12 zucchini blossoms
9 oz. butternut-squash meat
4 medium-sized zucchini
½ quart corn oil
Salt

Preparation

The Batter for the Shrimp: Combine the egg yolks with the flour in a bowl and mix well. Add the beer, and add salt to taste. Whip the egg whites until stiff, and incorporate them into the mixture.

The Batter for the Vegetables: Prepare as for the shrimp batter, using milk instead of the beer.

The Fry: Shell and devein the shrimp. Clean the zucchini blossoms. Cut the squash and the zucchini into sticks. Coat the vegetables with their batter, but dip the zucchini blossoms in carefully, one at a time. Heat the corn oil in a large frying pan, and fry the vegetables (they should be golden brown and crisp). Drain and dry on paper towels; then salt them sparingly. Dip the shrimp in their batter, fry them in the same oil, drain and dry on paper towels; then salt sparingly.

To Serve: Put a small paper napkin on each plate, and place the fry on top while still hot.

BUTTERNUT-SQUASH CAPPELLACCI, CUTTLEFISH

▼

Preparation Time: 3 hours

Ingredients for 6 Servings

For the Filling:

1 lb. butternut-squash meat
1 lemon
2 eggs
Nutmeg
⅓ cup ricotta cheese
⅓ cup salted ricotta cheese
2 slices white bread
without the crust
Salt and pepper

For the Sauce:

3 medium-sized cuttlefish
(available at Chinese markets)
½ onion
3 tablespoons extra
virgin olive oil
½ cup dry white wine
3½ oz. peeled tomatoes
Salt and pepper

For the Cappellacci Dough:

3¾ cups flour
6 eggs (1 egg will be
used to seal them)
Salt

Preparation

The Filling: Cut the butternut squash into chunks and discard the seeds. Place on a baking pan and cover with aluminum foil. Preheat the oven to 325°F, and cook for about 1 hour or until tender and dry. Allow to cool. Mash in a food processor and squeeze dry in a kitchen towel. In a bowl, add the grated lemon rind (being careful not to use the bitter white part), the egg yolks, some grated nutmeg, and all the other ingredients. Mix until well blended. Add salt and pepper to taste, and set aside.

The Sauce: Wash the cuttlefish, open them up carefully, and set aside the small ink bags (to do this, we recommend keeping the fresh fish for about 40 minutes in the freezer, so that the small ink bags will harden and become less fragile). Discard the snout and eyes. Cut the cuttlefish into thin strips. Chop the onion very fine, and brown in the olive oil in a nonstick skillet. Add the cuttlefish, let them brown, and douse with the wine. Let the wine evaporate; then add the tomatoes and the ink. Cook for about 45 minutes (if the mixture becomes too dry, add a little water). Add salt and pepper to taste if necessary, keeping in mind that the ink is already rather spicy. Keep warm.

The Butternut-Squash Cappellacci: Roll out a thin sheet of dough, and prepare the cappellacci (see Basic Recipes). Cook in plenty of salted water, and drain carefully.

To Serve: Serve on warm plates topped with sauce.

EEL, BUTTERNUT SQUASH, PUMPKIN SEEDS

▼

Preparation Time: 1 hour

Ingredients for 6 Servings

For the Pumpkin-Seed Sauce:
1 medium bunch of parsley
⅛ cup coriander seeds
⅓ cup pumpkin seeds
1 clove garlic
1 cup extra virgin olive oil
Juice of 1 lemon
Salt and pepper

For the Eels:
2 to 2½ lbs. of eels, skinned and cleaned
4 tablespoons extra virgin olive oil
Salt and pepper

For the Butternut-Squash Purée:
1 lb. butternut-squash meat
1 medium onion
½ cup butter
Salt
White and black pepper
Vegetable stock
(see Basic Recipes)
½ cup grated Parmesan cheese
1 stick cinnamon
Nutmeg

Preparation

The Pumpkin-Seed Sauce: Process all the ingredients in a blender. Set aside.

The Butternut-Squash Purée: Dice the squash and slice the onion thin. Brown the onion in a skillet with a pat of butter. Add the diced squash and salt and black pepper to taste, and bring slowly to a boil. (Add several spoonfuls of vegetable stock if the mixture becomes too dry.) Cook until done; then purée the squash in a food processor. In a bowl, add the rest of the butter and the Parmesan cheese, and mix thoroughly. Add a dash of white pepper and a little grated cinnamon and nutmeg. Keep warm.

The Eels: Fillet the eels. Rub them with the extra virgin olive oil, and cook them on the grill for about 5 minutes on each side. Add salt and pepper.

To Serve: Place the eel fillets still hot on individual plates, and top with the pumpkin-seed sauce at room temperature. Add a heaping spoonful of butternut-squash purée.

Candied Squash, Squash Ice Cream, Almond Wafers

▼

Preparation Time: 2 hours

Ingredients for 6 Servings

For the Squash Ice Cream:
1 lb. butternut-squash meat
½ quart milk
½ cup white sugar
1 vanilla bean
1 cinnamon stick
6 eggs
½ quart heavy cream

For the Almond Wafers:
3 cups flour
¾ cup almond flour
¼ cup sugar
½ teaspoon baking powder
Salt
½ quart milk
½ quart heavy cream
1½ cups butter, melted
8 eggs

In order to make the wafers, a pizelle iron is needed as well. It consists of two hinged metal plates. The plates have a diameter of about 6 to 8 inches and are embossed with small moulds that are generally round in shape.

For the Candied Squash: ⅔ cup candied squash (It takes a few days to make candied squash from fresh butternut squash. We describe the preparation in the Basic Recipes.)

Preparation

The Squash Ice Cream: Cut the butternut-squash meat into chunks, place on a baking pan, and cover with a sheet of aluminum foil. Preheat the oven to 325°F, and bake for about 1 hour or until it is quite tender. Remove from the oven, discard the seeds, and purée the squash in the food processor. Let it cool. Meanwhile, to make the cream mixture, combine the milk, the sugar, the vanilla bean (cut open lengthwise), and the cinnamon stick in a casserole. Place on a burner and bring to a boil.

Beat the egg yolks in a separate bowl, dilute with a little hot milk, and then add to the casserole. Place back on the burner until the mixture coats a spoon. Strain the cream through a fine sieve, and blend in a bowl with the heavy cream and the squash purée. Pour the mixture into an ice-cream machine.

The Almond Wafers: Combine the two types of flour, the sugar, baking powder, and a dash of salt in a saucepan. Add the milk, heavy cream, melted butter, and egg yolks. Beat 4 egg whites until stiff, and blend them into the mixture. Heat the waffle iron, and pour a ladleful of batter on one of the two plates. Close with the other plate, and turn over in such a manner that the mixture gets well distributed inside all of the small moulds. Let bake for about 4 minutes. Remove the wafers from the mould, place them on glasses turned upside down, and let them cool (this way, they will be shaped into small cups).

To Serve: Fill the small almond wafer cups with a heaping spoonful of squash ice cream. Place on individual plates, and sprinkle with the candied squash cut into very thin slices.

EMILIA ROMAGNA

Aceto Balsamico Tradizionale di Modena

Parmesan-Cheese Ice Cream, Pears, Aceto Balsamico Tradizionale di Modena

▼

Preparation Time: 45 minutes, plus 12 hours in the refrigerator

Ingredients for 6 Servings

For the Parmesan Cheese Ice Cream:
3 cups freshly grated Parmesan cheese
½ quart heavy cream
Black pepper

For the Garnish:
3 medium-sized pears
6 small clusters of champagne grapes (or a few red table grapes)
6 teaspoons Aceto Balsamico Tradizionale di Modena (Traditional Balsamic Vinegar of Modena)
1 short, oblong loaf of bread (¼ to ½ lb., unsliced)

Preparation

The Parmesan-Cheese Ice Cream: Place the grated Parmesan cheese in a stainless-steel bowl, and add the heavy cream a little at a time, stirring constantly. Melt the cheese in a double boiler, stirring continuously, until the mixture reaches a creamy consistency. Add a dash of pepper and mix well. Strain the mixture twice through a fine-mesh sieve. Pour the cream in a large, shallow container, and let cool in the refrigerator for about 12 hours.

The Garnish: Peel and core the pears, leaving the stems intact. Slice them through to the stalks and fan the slices. Then slice the bread and make crostini.

To Serve: Scoop the Parmesan-cheese ice cream onto individual plates, shaping it into a long oval with two spoons. Sprinkle with a teaspoon of Aceto Balsamico Tradizionale di Modena. Next to the ice cream, place the pear slices, a small cluster of grapes, and a few crostini.

Maccheroni "al Pettine," Zucchini Blossoms, Aceto Balsamico Tradizionale di Modena

▼

Preparation Time: 2 hours

Ingredients for 6 Servings

For the Sauce:
1 medium-sized red onion

2 slices prosciutto of about 3½ oz. each

⅓ cup butter

40 zucchini blossoms

12 teaspoons Aceto Balsamico Tradizionale di Modena (Traditional Balsamic Vinegar of Modena)

½ cup freshly grated Parmesan cheese

For the Maccheroni "al Pettine" (Hand-Made Penne):
3¾ cups flour

5 eggs

(To prepare this recipe, you need a *pettine*, which consists of a small wooden board with grooves that resembles a comb [*pettine*] and a small cylindrical stick. If this is unavailable, you can use a brand-new large comb and a pencil.)

Preparation

The Sauce: Cut the red onion in very fine slices. Then cut the prosciutto in thin slices. Brown the onion and prosciutto with half of the butter in a nonstick skillet for about 3 minutes. Remove from the burner and set aside.

The Maccheroni "al Pettine": Prepare a thin sheet of dough (see Basic Recipes), rolling it out on a clean surface. Cut small 1½-inch squares out of the dough. Roll the squares diagonally from the corner around the small wooden cylinder. Place on the *pettine*, pressing down with your fingers to create grooves in the dough. Slip the maccheroni off the stick, and set aside, dusting lightly with a little flour. Continue until all the dough is used up. Cook in plenty of salted boiling water, and drain when still slightly underdone. Reserve some cooking water.

To Serve: Sauté the prosciutto and the onion with the rest of the butter; then add the zucchini blossoms cut into four strips. Add the maccheroni "al pettine" (if the pasta becomes too dry, add a little of the salted water). Mix well and sprinkle with the Aceto Balsamico Tradizionale di Modena and the grated Parmesan cheese.

SNAILS, RED RADICCHIO LETTUCE, ACETO BALSAMICO TRADIZIONALE DI MODENA

▼

Preparation Time: 4 hours

Ingredients for 4 Servings

For the Snails:
48 snails, fresh only
1 fistful of coarse salt
1 cup dry white wine
1 carrot
1 onion
White peppercorns
1 bouquet garni
(see Basic Recipes)
Salt

For the Garnish:
4 slices of homemade bread
1 clove garlic

For the Sauce:
1 medium-sized red onion
1 tablespoon of extra virgin
olive oil
3½ oz. bacon
1 cup red wine
2 heads of red
radicchio lettuce
Salt and pepper
4 teaspoons Aceto
Balsamico Tradizionale di
Modena (Traditional Balsamic
Vinegar of Modena)

Preparation

The Snails: Put the live snails in a container, sprinkle with coarse salt, mix well, and place a lid on top. Purge them for 5 hours, and rinse with cold running water. Put them in a pan with cold water and bring to a boil. Drain them, remove them from their shells, and gut them. Prepare a cooking broth, using lightly salted water, the white wine, vegetables, whole peppercorns, and the bouquet garni. Cook the snails in the broth for about 3 hours, and let them cool in the broth.

The Sauce: Chop the onion very fine, and brown it in the extra virgin olive oil in a nonstick skillet. Finely slice the bacon, and combine with the onion. Add the red wine and snails, and cook over moderate heat for about 15 minutes to absorb the seasoning. Clean and wash the radicchio lettuce, slice it finely, and combine with the snails. Cook until the sauce is reduced by half, and add salt and pepper to taste. Remove from the heat, add the Aceto Balsamico Tradizionale di Modena, and mix well.

The Garnish: Toast the slices of bread in the oven, and rub them with the garlic.

To Serve: Serve the snails on warm plates and top with the sauce. Serve with a slice of toasted garlic bread.

Focaccia Bread, Almond Ice Cream, Strawberries, Aceto Balsamico Tradizionale di Modena

▼

Preparation Time: 2 hours

Ingredients for 4 Servings

For the Focaccia Bread:
3 tablespoons sugar
14 oz. heavy cream
Rind of 1 orange
3¾ cups flour
1 teaspoon baking powder
Salt

For the Almond Ice Cream:
1 vanilla bean
14 oz. heavy cream
14 oz. milk
15 egg yolks
1¼ cups sugar
¾ cup honey
1½ cups minced almonds

For the Strawberries:
32 medium-sized strawberries
4 teaspoons Aceto
Balsamico Tradizionale di
Modena (Traditional Balsamic
Vinegar of Modena)

Preparation

The Focaccia Bread: Melt 1 tablespoon of the sugar in a cup with 2 oz. of the fresh heavy cream, and set aside. Wash the orange, and cut the rind into very fine julienne, taking none of the white pith. Place in a stainless-steel bowl, add all the remaining ingredients, and mix well. Place the dough on a clean surface, and knead it well until it has a cylindrical shape with a diameter of about 2 inches. Cut it in slices about 1½ inches thick, and place them on a nonstick cookie sheet. Brush the top of each slice with the sugary cream. Place them in a preheated 350°F oven, and bake for about 30 minutes. Remove from the oven and let cool.

The Almond Ice Cream: Cut the vanilla bean open lengthwise, and place in a sauce pan together with the cream and the milk. Bring to a boil. Remove from the heat, add the egg yolks and sugar, and mix until the mixture is well blended. Strain through a sieve. Add the honey and place in the ice-cream machine. When the ice cream is ready (15 to 20 minutes), remove from the ice-cream machine and add the minced almonds. Mix well.

The Strawberries: Clean and wash the strawberries, cut them in half, and marinate them with the Aceto Balsamico Tradizionale di Modena for about 10 minutes.

To Serve: Cut the focaccia bread in half lengthwise, and place one half slice in the middle of each plate. Cover with the almond ice cream, and place the other half on top. Place the strawberries with their juice in a circle around the bread.

TUSCANY

Beans

PORK, BLACK-EYED BEANS

▼

Preparation Time: 2 hours, plus 6 hours to soak the beans

Ingredients for 4 Servings

For the Purée of Black-Eyed Beans:

1½ cups
dried black-eyed beans
½ carrot
½ onion
½ stalk of celery
1 clove garlic
6 tablespoons
extra virgin olive oil
(preferably from Tuscany)
10 parsley sprigs
Salt and pepper

For the Pork Patties:

1 potato
1 lb. boned pork shoulder
1 cup butter
Salt and pepper
1 egg
1 sprig rosemary
⅓ cup bread crumbs

For the Garnish:

4 tablespoons mustard

Preparation

The Purée of Black-Eyed Beans: Soak the dried beans in lukewarm water for about 6 hours. Slice the carrot, onion, and celery. Place the vegetables in a pan together with the clove of garlic, whole, and brown in the extra virgin olive oil. Drain the beans, add enough fresh water to cover them, and simmer until cooked (if the mixture should become too dry, add more water). Remove from the burner, and let cool slightly. Then add the parsley, and put three-fourths of the mixture through the food processor, saving one-fourth of the beans, whole. Collect the creamy mixture in a bowl. Add the whole beans, add salt and pepper to taste, and keep in a warm place.

The Pork Patties: Place the potato in a saucepan, and boil in lightly salted water until done. Remove and let cool. Trim and slice the pork shoulder. Brown the meat with ½ cup of butter in a cast-iron pan for about 10 minutes over moderate heat. Add salt and pepper to taste. Remove from the burner and let cool. Chop the meat very fine, and place in a bowl. Combine with the egg yolk, the rosemary leaves, finely chopped, and the potato, after discarding the peel. Add salt and pepper to taste. Mix well and shape into patties, using your hands. Coat them with bread crumbs, and fry in a nonstick skillet, using the remaining butter. Keep them warm.

To Serve: Place the lukewarm mashed-bean purée on individual plates, with the fried pork patties on top, and serve with a tablespoon of mustard.

POTATO AND BORLOTTI-BEAN RAVIOLI, BOTTARGA

▼

Preparation Time: 2 hours, plus 6 hours to soak the beans

Ingredients for 4 Servings

For the Filling:
¾ cup dried Borlotti beans
(brown Tuscan beans)
1 onion
½ carrot
½ celery stalk
2 cloves garlic
2 tablespoons of
extra virgin olive oil
(preferably from Tuscany)
1 medium-sized potato
2 sprigs thyme
2 oz. bacon
1½ cups freshly grated
Parmesan cheese
Salt and pepper

For the Ravioli Dough:
3 cups flour
4 eggs
Salt

For the Sauce:
⅓ cup butter
3 oz. bottarga (salted mullet
roe)

Preparation

The Filling: Soak the dried beans in lukewarm water for about 6 hours. Cut the onion, carrot, and celery into small chunks. Place in a pan together with a clove of garlic, whole, and brown in the olive oil. Drain the soaked beans, and add enough fresh water to cover them. Simmer for about 1 hour together with the vegetables (if the mixture becomes too dry, add more water). When done, put through a strainer and then through the food processor, collecting the mixture in a bowl. Boil the potato (it should be done, but not to the point where it falls apart), peel it, mash it in a potato masher, and combine it with the bean purée. Finely chop the thyme, remaining garlic clove, and bacon. Brown them slowly in a skillet. Add everything to the bean and potato mixture, ending with the grated Parmesan cheese. Then add salt and pepper to taste. Mix well with a wooden spoon, and let cool.

The Potato and Borlotti-Bean Ravioli: Prepare a thin sheet of dough and make the ravioli (see Basic Recipes). Cook in plenty of salted water, and drain well.

To Serve: Sauté the ravioli in the butter, using a nonstick skillet. Serve on warm plates, and top with very thin slices of bottarga.

LOBSTER, CANNELLINI BEANS

▼

Preparation Time: 2 hours, plus 6 hours to soak the beans

Ingredients for 4 Servings

For the Stew:

1½ cups
dried cannellini beans
1½ medium-sized potatoes
2 Roma tomatoes
1 sprig sage
1 sprig rosemary
2 cloves garlic
10 tablespoons
extra virgin olive oil
(preferably from Tuscany)
Salt and pepper
½ cup dry white wine

For the Lobster:

4 lobsters, 1⅛ lb. each
2 small
Roma tomatoes
2 shallots
2 tablespoons extra virgin
olive oil
20 leaves of fresh oregano
½ cup dry white wine

For the Garnish:

8 small sage leaves
Extra virgin olive oil
(preferably from Tuscany)
Black pepper

Preparation

The Stew: Soak the dried beans in lukewarm water for about 6 hours. Drain and set aside. Peel the potatoes, and dice together with the tomatoes. Combine in a skillet with the beans. Add the sage, the rosemary, the garlic cloves, whole, and 8 tablespoons of the extra virgin olive oil. Cook a few minutes over moderate heat to bring out the flavor, and add salt and pepper to taste. Add ½ cup of dry white wine, let evaporate, and add water to cover all the ingredients. Simmer over low heat for about 40 minutes or until the beans are tender but not overcooked. Remove half of the beans and the vegetables with a slotted spoon and set aside. Discard the garlic, and put everything else through the blender. Add the whole beans and the remaining extra virgin olive oil to the bean soup. Mix well and keep warm.

The Lobsters: Wash the lobsters, remove the claws, blanch them for about 5 minutes in boiling water, and remove the meat without breaking it apart. Set aside. Skin and dice the tomatoes. Finely chop the shallots. Cut the lobsters in half lengthwise. Sauté, meat side down, in a nonstick skillet with the olive oil and shallots. Add the fresh oregano, diced tomato, and the white wine. Let evaporate, remove the meat from the shells, and put it back into the skillet. Add the bean cream and cook over medium-high heat for about 5 minutes.

To Serve: Pour the stew in soup bowls and decorate with the claw meat and a few small sage leaves. Drizzle with a little extra virgin olive oil, and add a dash of freshly ground pepper.

BEANS, DRIED FRUIT

▼

Preparation Time: 2 hours, plus 6 hours to soak the beans

Ingredients for 10 Servings

For the Bean and Fruit Pound Cake:

¾ cup dried Borlotti beans (brown Tuscan beans)

6 walnuts

½ cup dates

7 medium-sized dried figs.

¾ cup dried apricots

1 cup raisins

3¾ cups flour

2 cups sugar

2 teaspoons baking powder

2 teaspoons baking soda

1 teaspoon cinnamon powder

6 cloves

Nutmeg

Salt

5 eggs

6 tablespoons milk

½ cup butter, softened

4 tablespoons extra virgin olive oil

1 teaspoon vanilla extract

1 lemon

⅓ cup honey

1 orange

For the Garnish:

½ pint vanilla ice cream (See Basic Recipes for our recipe for vanilla ice cream.)

Preparation

The Bean and Fruit Pound Cake: Soak the dried beans in lukewarm water for about 6 hours; then drain. Cook them in plenty of lightly salted fresh water, drain, put through the blender. Set aside. Mince the walnuts, dice the dried fruit, and combine in a bowl with 3 tablespoons of flour. Set aside. Combine the remaining flour in a bowl with the bean purée, sugar, baking powder, baking soda, cinnamon, cloves, a little ground nutmeg, and a dash of salt. Add the whole eggs, milk, butter, and olive oil, and mix well. Add as last ingredients the vanilla extract and the juice and grated rind of the lemon (being careful not to use the white part that has a bitter taste). Then add the dried fruit to the bean mixture, working it in with your hands. Use oven-proof wax paper to line a deep, rectangular cake pan, and pour the mixture in. Preheat the oven to 350°F, and bake the cake for about 1½ hours or until the top is nice and brown. Remove from the oven, and prick the top in several places with a fork. Combine the honey and the juice of an orange in a double boiler, and let them melt together. Pour the mixture over the cake so that it penetrates inside. Let cool and remove the cake from the pan.

To Serve: Cut the pound cake in slices, and place on individual plates. Serve with a heaping spoonful of vanilla ice cream.

UMBRIA

Black Truffle

PARTRIDGE, POTATOES, BLACK TRUFFLES, RADISHES

▼

Preparation Time: 1 hour

Ingredients for 4 Servings

For the Potato Salad:
4 medium-sized potatoes
1 small red onion
2 tablespoons mustard
1 egg yolk
3 tablespoons red wine vinegar
1 cup corn oil
Salt and pepper

For the Partridge:
8 partridge breasts
½ cup butter
4 tablespoons extra virgin olive oil
Salt and pepper

For the Garnish:
1¾ oz. fresh black truffles from Norcia
4 radishes

Preparation

The Potato Salad: Wash the potatoes, place them in a casserole with cold water to which a little salt has been added, place on the burner, and bring to a boil. Cook them until they are done; drain and let cool. Meanwhile, chop the onion very fine and mix with the mustard, egg yolk, and red wine vinegar. Add salt to taste, and cook the mixture in a double boiler, adding the corn oil a little at a time. Remove the mixture from the burner once it has reached a creamy consistency. Peel the potatoes, cut them in small round slices, and arrange on a platter. Sprinkle them with the sauce, and let them marinate for about 20 minutes.

The Partridge: Wash the partridge breasts. Let the butter and the oil sizzle in a cast-iron skillet; then brown the breasts over moderate heat on both sides. Add salt and pepper to taste; keep the meat in a warm place.

To Serve: Arrange the marinated potatoes on individual plates. Cut the truffles and the radishes into thin slices; then spread them over the potatoes. Place the partridge breasts on top while still hot.

Green Maccheroni, Cauliflower, Foie Gras, Black Truffles

▼

Preparation Time: 2 hours

Ingredients for 6 Servings

For the Cauliflower:
1 cauliflower of about 1 lb.
4 tablespoons extra virgin olive oil
Salt and pepper

For the Foie Gras:
8 oz. goose foie gras
Salt and pepper

For the Green Maccheroni:
1 lb. dried small-sized green maccheroni
2 tablespoons butter
Salt

For the Garnish:
¾ oz. fresh black truffles (preferably from Norcia)

Preparation

The Cauliflower: Discard the external leaves of the cauliflower, break off the florets, and cut them into small pieces that are no larger than the small-sized green maccheroni. Blanch them in salted boiling water; then drain and let dry on a kitchen towel. Heat the extra virgin olive oil in a skillet, and sauté the cauliflower. Add salt and pepper to taste, and put aside.

The Foie Gras: Soak the foie gras in lukewarm water for half an hour. Then take it out, and remove the skin and veins. Cut it into small ¼-inch cubes. Sauté them in a nonstick skillet, without adding butter or oil, until they are brown. Add salt and pepper.

The Green Maccheroni: Cook the maccheroni in plenty of boiling salted water, and drain when slightly underdone.

To Serve: Sauté the maccheroni in the skillet with the cauliflower florets; add the butter, then the foie gras. Serve on individual heated plates, and sprinkle with shaved black truffles.

Quail, Porcini Mushrooms, Savoy Cabbage, Black Truffles

▼

Preparation Time: 1 hour

Ingredients for 4 Servings

For the Porcini Mushrooms:
- 1 lb. porcini mushrooms
- 5 tablespoons extra virgin olive oil
- 1 clove garlic
- 1 sprig rosemary
- Salt

For the Savoy Cabbage:
- 8 oz. savoy cabbage (about ½ head)
- 3 tablespoons extra virgin olive oil
- 1 clove garlic
- 2 tablespoons red wine vinegar
- Salt

For the Quail:
- 8 quail, cleaned
- Salt and pepper
- 8 bay leaves
- 8 slices of bacon
- 2 tablespoons extra virgin olive oil
- ½ cup butter
- ½ cup white wine (preferably Trebbiano d'Abruzzo)
- ½ cup veal stock (see Basic Recipes)
- 3½ oz. fresh black truffles (preferably from Norcia)

Preparation

The Porcini Mushrooms: Clean the mushrooms with a small brush, wipe with a damp cloth, and cut in thin slices. Add the extra virgin olive oil to a nonstick skillet, and brown the garlic clove, whole. Add the mushrooms together with the rosemary sprig and sauté. Add salt to taste, and keep in a warm place.

The Savoy Cabbage: Open the cabbage, discard the tough outer leaves, and blanch the others. Let dry on a clean kitchen towel. Add the extra virgin olive oil to a skillet, and sauté the cabbage together with the garlic clove, whole. Add the vinegar and let cook to evaporate. Add salt to taste, and keep warm.

The Quail: Salt and pepper the insides of the quail, and place a bay leaf inside each. Wrap them in the bacon slices. Heat the extra virgin olive oil in a skillet with ¼ cup of the butter, and brown on both sides. Place them for about 7 minutes in an oven preheated to 375° to 400°F. Remove, and let rest in a warm place. Degrease the quail juices, add the white wine, veal stock, and remaining butter, and simmer until reduced by half. Chop the black truffles, and add to the sauce.

To Serve: Arrange the savoy cabbage and porcini mushrooms on individual plates. Place the hot quail on top, and drizzle the cooking juices over them.

ZABAGLIONE, BLACK TRUFFLES

▼

Preparation Time: 15 minutes, plus 24 hours to acquire the flavor

Ingredients for 6 Servings

For the Zabaglione:
3½ oz. fresh black truffles (preferably from Norcia)
6 eggs
6 tablespoons sugar
4 tablespoons Marsala Vergine wine

For the Garnish:
12 small dry cookies

Preparation

The Zabaglione: Let the eggs (in their shells) absorb the flavor of the black truffles by placing them together in a tightly closed glass container. Seal and leave in the refrigerator for 24 hours. Then remove the eggs from the container, break them, and separate the yolks from the whites. Combine the yolks, the sugar, and the Marsala Vergine wine in a metal bowl (copper is best). Mix until well blended. Place the bowl in a double boiler, and beat the mixture with a whisk for about 10 minutes. (For an excellent zabaglione, make sure that the water in the double boiler does not reach the boiling point.)

To Serve: Serve the zabaglione hot in individual dessert bowls. Serve with small dry cookies.

MARCHE

Pecorino Cheese

EGGPLANT, PINE NUTS, PECORINO CHEESE

▼

Preparation Time: 1 hour

Ingredients for 4 Servings

For the Eggplant:
8 medium-sized eggplants
1 clove garlic
5 tablespoons extra virgin olive oil
Vegetable stock (see Basic Recipes)
⅔ cup tomato sauce (see Basic Recipes)
⅓ cup pine nuts
Salt and pepper

For the Garnish:
3½ oz. young Pecorino cheese (sheep's milk cheese)

Preparation

The Eggplant: Wash the eggplants and scoop out most of the pulp, leaving a thick shell. Discard the pulp, and cut the shell into strips. Brown the garlic clove whole in the extra virgin olive oil, and add the eggplant strips. Cook for 30 minutes over moderate heat, adding some of the vegetable stock from time to time. When halfway done, add the tomato sauce and the whole pine nuts. Season with salt and pepper.

To Serve: Serve the eggplant on individual plates. Top with the Pecorino cheese cut into thin slices.

ZITI, PECORINO CHEESE, PANCETTA, FAVA BEANS

▼

Preparation Time: 90 minutes

Ingredients for 4 Servings

For the Sauce:
2¼ lbs. fava beans (in their shells)
3½ oz. pancetta
2 tablespoons extra virgin olive oil
1 spring onion, chopped
1 cup chicken stock (see Basic Recipes)
2 tablespoons butter
Salt and pepper

For the Ziti:
12 oz. dried ziti
Salt

For the Garnish:
2 oz. aged Pecorino cheese (sheep's milk cheese), grated

Preparation

The Sauce: Shell the beans, and remove the thin external skin as well (to simplify this procedure, blanch them in boiling water and then cool in ice water). Dice the pancetta, and brown in a skillet with the extra virgin olive oil. Add the chopped onion and the fava beans. Heat the chicken stock, and pour over the mixture. Add salt and pepper. Let cook to absorb the seasoning and keep warm. (The cooking time depends on the size of the beans.)

The Ziti: Cook the ziti in plenty of boiling salted water, and drain when they are still slightly underdone. Reserve some of the water.

To Serve: Heat the fava beans in a skillet. Add the ziti and sauté them, adding the butter at the end (if they become too dry, add some of the reserved water). Serve on warm plates with a little sauce on top, and sprinkle with the grated Pecorino cheese.

CHICKEN, SUN-DRIED TOMATOES, LEEKS, PECORINO CHEESE

▼

Preparation Time: 1 hour

Ingredients for 4 Servings

For the Fried Leeks:
4 medium-sized leeks
1 cup corn oil
Salt

For the Chicken:
8 sun-dried tomatoes in oil
7 oz. young Pecorino cheese (sheep's milk cheese), grated
4 chicken breasts
Flour
5 tablespoons extra virgin olive oil
½ cup dry white wine
1 lemon
2 sprigs thyme
¼ cup butter
Salt and pepper

Preparation

The Fried Leeks: Wash the leeks carefully to rid them of grit, discarding the tough outer leaves. Cut the leeks into thin strips, and fry in the corn oil until crisp and golden. Drain and dry on paper towels. Add salt to taste.

The Chicken: Cut the tomatoes into thin strips, and place in a bowl. Mix in the grated Pecorino cheese, and set aside. Open the chicken breasts, and cut them in half. Place each half between two pieces of clear plastic wrap, and pound them with a meat pounder into the shape of thin cutlets. Remove from the plastic wrap, and place a fourth of the tomato mixture on each cutlet. Shape each into a roll, and tie with kitchen string. Dust with flour, and brown them in the olive oil over moderate heat in an oven-proof skillet. Then place in a pre-heated 375° to 400°F oven, and bake for about 15 minutes. When almost done, baste them with the white wine. Remove the skillet from the oven, and put the chicken rolls in a warm place. Reduce the sauce, add the lemon juice and thyme, add salt and pepper to taste, and thicken with the butter.

To Serve: Remove the string from the chicken rolls, and slice them diagonally. Place the slices on warmed individual plates, and top with the sauce and some of the fried leeks.

Pecorino Cheese, Honey, Pears

▼

Preparation Time: 15 minutes

Ingredients for 4 Servings

4 William pears
10½ oz. fresh Pecorino cheese (sheep's milk cheese)
5 tablespoons honey

Preparation

Wash the pears. Cut them into thin slices and set aside. Cut the Pecorino cheese into thin slices and set aside. Melt the honey in a double boiler and keep warm.

To Serve: Arrange the pear and Pecorino cheese slices in a circle on each plate, topping with the melted honey.

ABRUZZI

Saffron

MUSSELS, PEPPERS, SAFFRON

▼

Preparation Time: 45 minutes

Ingredients for 4 Servings

For the Mussels:
32 mussels
2 cloves garlic (pressed for juice, but left whole)
½ cup extra virgin olive oil
½ cup dry white wine
White pepper
¼ teaspoon saffron threads
Salt

For the Peppers:
2 yellow peppers

Preparation

The Mussels: Wash and clean the mussels in cold running water. Sauté them with the garlic in a skillet in the extra virgin olive oil. Place a lid on the skillet and cook the mussels until all have opened up. Remove them from the skillet, and keep them at room temperature. Add the white wine to the cooking liquid and white pepper to taste. Heat for about 2 minutes to reduce the wine. Put the liquid through a fine-mesh strainer, and heat again, while adding the saffron and salt to taste. Reduce the sauce 5 more minutes and keep warm.

The Peppers: Roast the yellow peppers over high heat on all sides for about 10 minutes. Cool them in cold water, skin and dry them, and cut them into very thin slices.

To Serve: Discard the top shells, and divide the mussels among four soup bowls. Top them with the yellow pepper slices, and add some of the hot sauce.

MALTAGLIATI, SAFFRON, SPINY LOBSTER, PORCINI MUSHROOMS

▼

Preparation Time: 2 hours

Ingredients for 4 Servings

For the Sauce:
1 spiny lobster, about 2¼ lbs.
2 medium-sized porcini mushrooms
6 tablespoons extra virgin olive oil
2 cloves garlic
3 tablespoons butter
1 shallot
½ cup of dry white wine
Salt and pepper

For the Maltagliati Dough:
3 cups flour
4 eggs
½ teaspoon of saffron threads
Salt

For the Garnish:
10 Italian parsley leaves

Preparation

The Sauce: Put the live lobster in a pan with boiling water, and cook it for about 10 minutes. Drain and let cool. Clean the porcini mushrooms, and cut the caps only in slices. In a skillet, brown the garlic cloves whole in 3 tablespoons of olive oil. Add the mushrooms and sauté. Carefully remove the meat from the lobster shell, and cut into about ½"-inch-thick medallions. Keep warm.

The Maltagliati: Prepare the pasta dough (see Basic Recipes), adding the saffron in the beginning, together with the eggs. Roll out into a thin sheet on a clean surface, and let dry slightly. Shape the maltagliati (see Basic Recipes). Cook in plenty of boiling salted water, and drain while still slightly underdone. Reserve some of the water.

To Serve: Let the butter sizzle in a skillet with the chopped shallot. Add the white wine and reduce. Add the lobster medallions and porcini mushrooms, and sauté lightly, adding salt and pepper to taste (if they get too dry, add a little of the salted water). Pour the maltagliati into the skillet, and heat a while to absorb the seasoning. Serve on warmed plates, and sprinkle with chopped parsley. Drizzle the remaining extra virgin olive oil over the pasta.

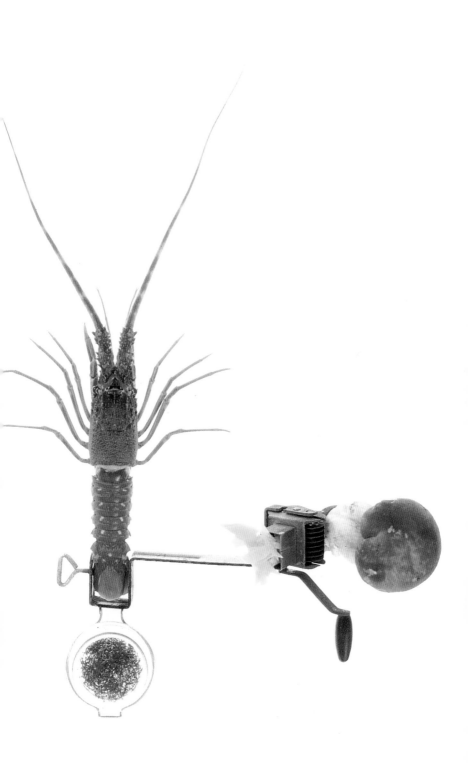

SWORDFISH, ONIONS, TREBBIANO D'ABRUZZO WINE, SAFFRON

▼

Preparation Time: 30 minutes

Ingredients for 4 Servings

For the Sauce:

8 green onions
2 tablespoons extra virgin olive oil
¼ cup butter
½ cup dry white wine
1 cup fish stock (see Basic Recipes)
½ teaspoon saffron threads
4 sage leaves
1 lemon
Salt and pepper

For the Swordfish:

2 cloves garlic
4 tablespoons bread crumbs
3 tablespoons extra virgin olive oil
Salt and pepper
4 swordfish steaks, 6 to 7 oz. each

For the Garnish:

2 small tomatoes

Preparation

The Sauce: Clean and chop the green onions. Brown in the extra virgin olive oil and butter in a skillet. Add white wine and reduce. Add the fish stock, saffron, sage leaves, and lemon juice. Cook over medium-high heat until the sauce is reduced by half. Add salt and pepper to taste. Keep warm.

The Swordfish: Mince the garlic, and mix it in with the bread crumbs and 1 tablespoon of the extra virgin olive oil in a bowl. Salt and pepper the fish steaks, bread them, and brown in a nonstick skillet greased with the remaining olive oil. Continue to cook the fish until the surface is nicely browned.

To Serve: Serve the swordfish steaks on warmed plates together with a little of the sauce and with a few tomato slices as garnish.

Vanilla Fritters, Orange-Blossom Water, Saffron

Preparation Time: 1 hour

Ingredients for 4 Servings

For the Vanilla Fritters:
½ teaspoon saffron threads
½ cup orange-blossom water
½ cup butter
Salt
1 vanilla bean
2¼ cups flour
¾ cup sugar
3 eggs
1 quart corn oil

Preparation

The Vanilla Fritters: Soak the saffron threads in the orange-blossom water. Melt the butter in a saucepan together with ½ cup of water. Add a dash of salt and the vanilla bean (cut open lengthwise), and bring to a boil. Remove from the burner; then add the flour a little at a time and ½ cup of the sugar. Mix with a whisk until well blended. Place the saucepan back on the burner, and cook until smooth and creamy. Blend in the whole eggs and saffron with the orange-blossom water. Mix well, remove from the heat, and let stand until lukewarm. Discard the vanilla bean, place the mixture in a pastry bag, and squeeze out small rings of pastry directly into a skillet of hot oil. Fry the fritters until they float to the top and are beautifully browned. Remove with a slotted spoon, drain, and dry on paper towels.

To Serve: Sprinkle the vanilla fritters with the remaining sugar, and serve on a tray while still hot.

MOLISE

Wheat

Pizza Rustica, Pork, Raisins

Preparation Time: 1 hour, plus 24 hours to soak the wheat berries and 2 hours to let the dough rise

Ingredients for 6 Servings

For the Pizza Rustica:

1 oz. wheat berries
1 to 2 tablespoons raisins
1 cup fresh pork cracklings
3¾ cups flour
1 oz. yeast (2 envelopes dry yeast)
8 tablespoons extra virgin olive oil
3 eggs
½ teaspoon salt
Butter (for the pizza pan)

Preparation

The Wheat: Soak the wheat berries in lukewarm water for about 24 hours. Drain and cook in plenty of lightly salted water until tender. Drain and set aside.

The Pizza Rustica: Soften the raisins in lukewarm water for about 30 minutes. Drain and carefully squeeze out all the water in a kitchen towel. Finely chop the pork cracklings. Place the flour on a thoroughly clean surface, and make a well in the middle. Dissolve the yeast in 1 cup of lukewarm water, and pour it into the well with all the other ingredients. Mix with your hands and knead well until the dough is soft and elastic. Lightly grease a pizza pan about 1½ inches deep; then thin and stretch the dough to fit the pan evenly. Let rise in a warm place for about 2 hours. Bake the pizza in a preheated 375° to 400°F oven for about half an hour or until the surface is golden brown and crisp. Remove from the oven, and cut in rectangles while still hot.

To Serve: Serve the pizza on a tray covered with a napkin.

WHEAT, PORK, WILD FENNEL

▼

Preparation Time: 3 hours, plus 24 hours to soak the wheat berries

Ingredients for 6 Servings

For the Wheat Soup:

1 lb. wheat berries

1 carrot

1 stalk celery

1 onion

3 San Marzano tomatoes (or Roma tomatoes)

5 oz. smoked pork jowl or pancetta

1 clove garlic

2 to 3 medium-sized potatoes

5 tablespoons extra virgin olive oil

2 quarts chicken stock (see Basic Recipes)

Salt and pepper

⅔ oz. fresh wild fennel (or ⅓ oz. if dried)

Preparation

The Wheat Soup: Soak the wheat berries in lukewarm water for about 24 hours. Thinly slice the carrot, celery, onion, and tomatoes. Chop the smoked pork and the garlic. Cut the potatoes into small cubes, and cover with water to keep them from turning color. Place a pan on a burner that is big enough to hold the soup. Add 3 tablespoons of extra virgin olive oil, and brown the vegetables together with the smoked pork. Drain the wheat berries and potatoes, and add to the browned vegetables. Let them absorb the seasoning, and then add the chicken stock. Cook for about 1 hour or until the wheat berries are tender. Use a strainer to remove half of the wheat berries together with the vegetables, and set aside. Put the rest through a food processor. Now combine the wheat berries and the vegetables with the processed mixture, and place on the stove. Bring to a boil, add salt and pepper to taste, and let cook for about 15 minutes, while stirring with a wooden spoon. Before removing the soup from the burner, add two tablespoons of the extra virgin olive oil and season with wild fennel.

The Serve: Pour the wheat soup into individual soup bowls, adding just a little extra virgin olive oil.

RED SNAPPER, BREAD, CUMIN

▼

Preparation Time: 90 minutes, plus 2 hours to let the dough rise

Ingredients for 8 Servings

For the Red Snapper:

1 lemon

1 red snapper,
about 4½ lbs., cleaned

1 sprig rosemary

1 sprig thyme

4 bay leaves

Salt and pepper

For the Bread Crust:

8 cups wheat flour

1¾ oz. yeast
(3½ envelopes dry yeast)

½ teaspoon sugar

4 tablespoons extra virgin
olive oil

2 teaspoons salt

1 tablespoon cumin seeds

1 egg

½ cup milk

Preparation

The Red Snapper: Cut the lemon in slices, and place inside the fish with the rosemary, thyme, and bay leaves. Sprinkle with salt and pepper.

The Bread Crust: Place the flour on a smooth, thoroughly clean surface, and make a well in the middle. Dissolve the yeast and the sugar in 1 cup of lukewarm water, and then pour this mixture in the well, together with the extra virgin olive oil and the salt. Mix with your hands and knead well until the dough is soft and elastic. Place the dough in a lightly floured bowl, and make a cross-shaped cut in the top surface. Cover with a clean kitchen towel, and let rise in a warm place for about two hours or until the dough has risen to at least twice its size. Place the dough on a floured surface, add the cumin seeds, and knead until the dough is puffed up and elastic. Divide the dough in half, and roll out two oval-shaped sheets about ¼ inch thick.

The Red Snapper in the Bread Crust: Line a baking pan with wax paper, and place one of the oval-shaped sheets of dough on it. Place the fish in the middle, cover with the other sheet of dough, and press together all around, following the shape of the fish. Cut away the excess dough with a serrated cutting wheel. Use the point of a knife to make several cuts resembling the scales of a fish in the top sheet of dough, so as to facilitate the escape of steam that will form during cooking. Brush the surface with the egg wash. Bake the fish in a preheated 475°F oven for about ½ hour to 40 minutes or until the bread crust turns a golden brown.

To Serve: Serve the fish in the bread crust on a serving platter.

WHEAT, WALNUTS, CHOCOLATE

▼

Preparation Time: 2 hours, plus 24 hours to soak the wheat berries

Ingredients for 4 Servings

For the Wheat Berries:
7 oz. wheat berries
Salt

For the Wheat Berries Compote:
1 tablespoon sugar
3½ oz. dark chocolate
16 walnuts
4 sprigs red currants (or small raisins)
Cooked wine (see Basic Recipes)

Preparation

The Wheat Berries: Soak the wheat berries in lukewarm water for about 24 hours; drain. Cook in plenty of lightly salted water until tender. Drain again. Place in a bowl together with the sugar, mix, and let cool.

The Wheat Berries Compote: Shave the dark chocolate into flakes. Coarsely chop the walnuts. Clean and wash the red currants (or the raisins). Combine everything with the wheat berries, and add as much cooked wine as necessary to make a smooth consistency. Mix carefully.

To Serve: Serve the wheat compote in individual dessert bowls.

LATIUM

Ricotta Cheese

RICOTTA CHEESE, PANCETTA, DANDELION GREENS, POPPY SEEDS

▼

Preparation Time: 1 hour

Ingredients for 4 Servings

For the Ricotta Pies:
2 oz. pancetta
3½ oz. dandelion greens
1¾ oz. Parmesan cheese (about ½ cup grated)
8 eggs
⅔ cup ricotta cheese
⅓ oz. poppy seeds
Salt and pepper

For Buttering the Bowls:
¼ cup butter
3 tablespoons bread crumbs
(To make this recipe, you will also need 4 terracotta bowls that can hold about 7 oz.)

Preparation

The Ricotta Pies: Cut the pancetta into small cubes, and fry until crisp in a skillet without adding oil or butter. Clean and wash the dandelion greens; finely chop and blanch them. Grate the Parmesan cheese. Place the eggs in a container and beat with a whisk. Add the ricotta cheese and poppy seeds, and mix well. Add salt and pepper. Butter the terracotta bowls, sprinkle them with bread crumbs, pour the mixture in, and place in a preheated 375° to 400°F oven. Bake until the pies are puffed up and golden brown.

To Serve: Serve the ricotta pies at once in the bowls in which they were baked.

RICOTTA, FAVA-BEAN, AND THYME TORTELLONI

▼

Preparation Time: 2 hours

Ingredients for 4 Servings

For the Filling:
1½ lbs. fresh fava beans
(with the shell)
3½ oz. prosciutto
2 shallots
3 tablespoons extra virgin
olive oil
¼ cup vegetable stock
(see Basic Recipes)
1¼ cups ricotta cheese
1 cup freshly grated
Parmesan cheese
2 eggs
Salt and pepper
Bread crumbs (not from
the crust of the bread)

For the Sauce:
½ lb. fresh fava beans
(with the shell)
¼ cup butter
3 sprigs fresh thyme
¼ cup grated Parmesan cheese

For the Tortelloni Dough:
2 cups flour
5 eggs (1 egg will be used
to seal them)
Salt

Preparation

The Filling: Shell all the fava beans (including the ones for the sauce). Blanch in salted boiling water for 1 minute, drain, and put them in ice water to stop the cooking process. Remove the thin outer skin from the beans, and set aside a quarter of them to be used for the sauce. Finely chop the prosciutto and shallots, and brown them in a skillet with the extra virgin olive oil. Add the rest of the fava beans and the vegetable stock, and cook for about 5 minutes. Remove the skillet from the burner, and let stand until lukewarm. Save the cooking liquid. Chop the fava beans with a knife, and put them in a bowl. Add the ricotta, grated Parmesan cheese, 2 egg yolks, and salt and pepper to taste. Mix well. If the consistency of the mixture is too soft, thicken with some bread crumbs.

The Sauce: Combine the butter with 1 cup of the bean cooking liquid in a saucepan, and reduce by half. Add the beans that were set aside earlier as well as a few small leaves of fresh thyme, and let cook to absorb the seasoning. Keep warm.

The Ricotta Tortelloni: Roll out a thin paste of dough and prepare the tortelloni (see Basic Recipes). Cook in plenty of salted water, and drain carefully. Reserve some of the water.

To Serve: Combine the tortelloni with the sauce, and sauté about 2 minutes (if they get too dry, add some of the salted water). Place on warmed plates, and sprinkle with Parmesan.

VEAL, ZUCCHINI, RICOTTA CHEESE

▼

Preparation Time: 1 hour

Ingredients for 4 Servings

For the Zucchini:
2 medium-size zucchini
3 tablespoons flour
1 cup corn oil
Salt

For the Veal:
1½ lb. boneless veal loin
Salt
½ cup butter
½ cup dry white wine
7 oz. smoked ricotta cheese
1 sprig rosemary
Pepper

Preparation

The Zucchini: Wash and slice the zucchini, dust with flour, and fry in a skillet in the corn oil. Drain and dry on paper towels, and sprinkle with salt. Keep in a warm place.

The Veal: Lightly salt the veal, and brown in an oven-proof skillet in half the butter. Pour the white wine over the meat, and cook it in a preheated 475°F oven, until brown on the outside but soft and pink on the inside. Remove from the oven, slice, and place the cutlets on a buttered baking pan. Put the fried zucchini and the sliced ricotta over the meat, and cook until the cheese is melted. Remove from the oven, place on a tray, and keep in a warm place. Reduce the cooking liquid over high heat, thicken with the remaining ¼ cup of butter, and let it cook with the sprig of rosemary to absorb the seasoning. Add salt and pepper to taste.

To Serve: Top the veal cutlets with the sauce, and serve on individual plates.

BAKED CREAM WITH RICOTTA CHEESE

Preparation Time: 2 hours

Ingredients for 6 Servings

For the Baked Cream with Ricotta Cheese:

¾ cup sugar

½ quart milk

1 vanilla bean

3 cups ricotta cheese

10 eggs

1 teaspoon light brown sugar

Preparation

The Cream with Ricotta Cheese: In a saucepan, melt the sugar with the milk. Add the vanilla bean (cut open lengthwise). Remove from the heat. Remove the vanilla bean, scrape out the seeds with a knife and return them to the mixture. Add the ricotta cheese and egg yolks. Mix until well blended. Put the cream mixture through a medium-mesh strainer, and pour it into individual 3-inch bowls, about 1 inch deep. Cook the cream in a water bath in a preheated 300°F oven for about 90 minutes. Remove from the oven, and let stand until luke-warm. Place in the refrigerator until completely firm.

To Serve: Sprinkle the light brown sugar evenly over the top of the cream, and place in a salamander until the sugar is caramelized. Let cool for a few minutes before serving. (If no salamander is available, the direct flame of a propane torch can also be used to caramelize the surface.)

CAMPANIA

Tomato

White Onions, Tomatoes, Sun-Dried Tomatoes, Black Olives

▼

Preparation Time: 4 hours

Ingredients for 6 Servings

For the Tomatoes:
6 medium-sized
round tomatoes
Salt
1 tablespoon sugar
2 sprigs rosemary
4 sprigs thyme
2 cloves garlic

For the Onions:
4 white onions
2 cups white wine vinegar
1 cup sugar
4 bay leaves
Salt
Black peppercorns
6 tablespoons extra virgin
olive oil
2 sprigs thyme

For the Garnish:
3 sun-dried tomatoes
24 black Italian olives
12 basil leaves
Salt and pepper

Preparation

The Tomatoes: Wash and dry the tomatoes. Cut them in half, and discard the seeds. Place them cut side up on a sheet pan, and sprinkle with salt and sugar, then with the rosemary and thyme leaves, and, finally, with the garlic cut into thin slivers. Cook them in a preheated 200°F oven for about 3 hours. Remove them from the oven, let cool, and skin them carefully by hand.

The Onions: Clean, peel, and slice the onions. Place a pan with 2 cups of water on the burner. Add the onions, and mix in the white wine vinegar, sugar, bay leaves, a dash of salt, and some black peppercorns. Bring to a boil, and let cook for about 5 minutes. Remove from the heat. Add the extra virgin olive oil and thyme leaves. Let marinate for about 30 minutes.

To Serve: Coarsely chop the baked tomatoes; then place them on individual plates, and cover with the marinated onions. Cut the sun-dried tomatoes in thin slices, and place on top of the onions together with the pitted black olives and basil leaves. Add salt and pepper to taste. (You can add slices of toasted garlic bread.)

SPAGHETTI ALLA CHITARRA, TOMATOES, SEA URCHIN ROE

▼

Preparation Time: 2 hours

Ingredients for 6 Servings

For the Sauce:
20 sea urchin roe
6 tablespoons extra virgin olive oil
½ lemon
10 to 11 oz. tomatoes (red and green ones)
2 tablespoons chopped parsley
Salt and pepper

For the Spaghetti alla Chitarra (Shaped on the Guitar):
3¾ cups flour
5 eggs
Salt

(To make this recipe, you will need a tool called a "guitar" for its resemblance to the musical instrument. It consists of a rectangular wooden frame about 8 × 15 inches upon which very thin steel wires are stretched.)

Preparation

The Sauce: Place the sea urchin roe in a very large bowl. Add the extra virgin olive oil and the juice of ½ lemon. Beat with a whisk. Dice the tomatoes, discarding the seeds. Add the tomato cubes to the mixture together with the parsley. Add salt and pepper to taste.

The Spaghetti alla Chitarra (Shaped on the Guitar): Roll out a sheet of dough (see Basic Recipes), as thick as the distance between the wires of the guitar (about ⅛ inch). Leave the dough on a clean surface in a dry place for about 20 minutes. Now cut the dough into rectangles to fit the size of the guitar, and place these one at a time on the steel wires. Move the rolling pin over them back and forth, pressing hard so as to obtain spaghetti with squared edges. Continue to do this until the dough is used up. Cook the spaghetti in plenty of boiling salted water, and drain when slightly underdone.

To Serve: Combine the spaghetti and the sauce, mix well, and serve on warmed plates. (If the pasta is too dry, add a little extra virgin olive oil.)

OCTOPUS, CELERY, TOMATOES

▼

Preparation Time: 90 minutes

Ingredients for 4 Servings

For the Octopus:
Salt
1 onion
1 carrot
1 celery stalk
8 tablespoons white wine vinegar
4 bay leaves
20 black peppercorns
3 to 3½ lbs. octopus legs

For the Tomatoes:
4 San Marzano tomatoes (or Roma tomatoes)
1 celery stalk
1 small sprig of parsley
Juice of 1 lemon
Salt and pepper

For the Garnish:
6 tablespoons extra virgin olive oil

Preparation

The Octopus: Place a deep pot with three quarts of lightly salted water on the burner. Dice the onion, carrot, and 1 of the celery stalks, and add to the pot with the white wine vinegar, whole bay leaves, and black peppercorns. Bring to a boil. Add the octopus and cook until tender. Remove from the pot and set aside. Cut the octopus, including the tentacles, into small pieces.

The Tomatoes: Blanch the tomatoes in boiling water. Then place in ice water to stop the cooking process. Skin, discard the seeds, and chop coarsely. Finely dice the remaining celery stalk, and chop the parsley. Place in a bowl together with the tomatoes and the octopus. Season with the juice of the lemon and with salt and pepper. Mix carefully.

To Serve: Place the octopus with the vegetables on individual plates, adding a little extra virgin olive oil to each plate.

SWEET RAVIOLI, GREEN TOMATOES

▼

Preparation Time: 90 minutes, plus 20 hours to soak the tomatoes and 4 hours to make the marmalade

Ingredients for 4 Servings

For the Green-Tomato Marmalade:
2¼ lbs green tomatoes
2 cups sugar
4 lemons

For the Sweet-Ravioli Short Pastry:
1½ cups flour
1 egg
½ cup sugar
⅓ cup butter
1 teaspoon baking powder
Grated rind of 1 lemon
1 egg yolk and ½ cup milk (for the egg wash)

For the Garnish:
2 tablespoons of confectioners' sugar

Preparation

The Green-Tomato Marmalade: Wash and dice the tomatoes, discarding the seeds. Place the tomatoes in a stainless-steel casserole together with the sugar and the grated lemon rind (be careful not to use the white part that has a bitter taste). Let them soak in a cool place for about 20 hours. When they are finished soaking, place the casserole on the burner and cook the marmalade for about 4 hours, stirring often with a wooden spoon. Remove from the heat and let cool.

The Sweet Ravioli: Prepare the short pastry (see Basic Recipes). Use a lightly floured rolling pin to roll it out on a clean surface to a ⅛-inch thickness. Cut the dough into 2½-inch disks with a round pastry cutter. Prepare the ravioli by placing a teaspoon of the tomato marmalade in the middle of each little disk. Close them by overlapping the edges of the dough, and brush the surface with the egg wash. Place them on a cookie sheet lined with wax paper, and bake in a preheated 350°F oven for about 20 minutes or until golden brown.

To Serve: Place the sweet ravioli still warm on a tray, and sprinkle with confectioners' sugar.

APULIA

Chickpeas

CUTTLEFISH EGGS, CHICKPEAS

▼

Preparation Time: 2 hours, plus 12 hours to soak the chickpeas

Ingredients for 4 Servings:

For the Chickpeas:
1 cup dried chickpeas
1 celery stalk
1 carrot
1 stalk Swiss chard
4 bay leaves
Salt and pepper

For the Cuttlefish Eggs:
½ cup fish stock (see Basic Recipes)
1 lb. cuttlefish eggs (available at Japanese markets)
Extra virgin olive oil (preferably from Apulia)
Pepper

Preparation

The Chickpeas: Soak the chickpeas in lukewarm water for about 12 hours. Drain them. Combine the soaked chickpeas with the coarsely chopped vegetables, add bay leaves, and cook in boiling, lightly salted water for about 1 hour or until the chickpeas are tender. Remove them from the water, and keep warm.

The Cuttlefish Eggs: Bring the fish stock to a boil in a skillet, and blanch the cuttlefish eggs for about 3 minutes.

To Serve: Ladle some of the cuttlefish eggs and the liquid in which they were cooked into each of the soup bowls, and add a heaping spoonful of chickpeas. Add salt and pepper to taste. Finish by adding a little extra virgin olive oil and some freshly ground pepper.

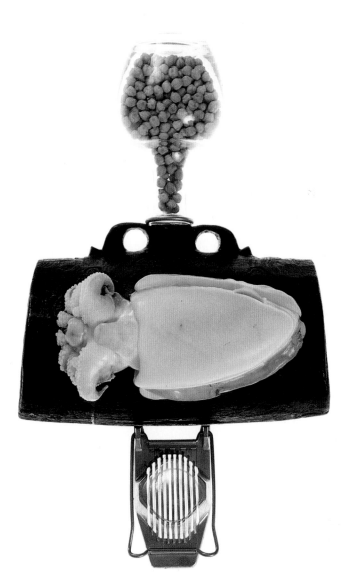

ORECCHIETTE, PRAWNS, CHICKPEAS, SAGE

▼

Preparation Time: 2 hours, plus 12 hours to soak the chickpeas

Ingredients for 4 Servings

For the Chickpeas:
½ cup dried chickpeas
1 celery stalk
1 carrot
2 bay leaves
Salt and pepper

For the Orecchiette:
11 oz. orecchiette
(ear-shaped pasta)
Extra virgin olive oil
(preferably from Apulia)
Salt

For the Prawns:
1 lb. prawns
1 clove garlic
1 shallot
2 tablespoons
extra virgin olive oil
(preferably from Apulia)
1 cup dry white wine
2 ripe tomatoes
8 sage leaves
Salt and pepper

Preparation

The Chickpeas: Soak the chickpeas in lukewarm water for about 12 hours. Drain. Combine with the coarsely chopped vegetables, add bay leaves, and simmer in lightly salted water for about 1 hour or until the chickpeas are tender. Remove from the burner, and let cool in the cooking liquid.

The Prawns: Shell, clean, and wash the prawns, keeping four with their heads on, to be used for garnish. Finely chop the garlic and the shallot, and brown in a nonstick skillet in the extra virgin olive oil. Add the prawns, and sauté for a few minutes. Douse with the wine, and let it evaporate. Add salt and pepper to taste.

The Orecchiette: Cook the orecchiette in plenty of salted water, and drain when slightly underdone. Reserve some of the water.

To Serve: Place the skillet with the prawns on the burner (keeping aside the four that will be used for garnish), and add the chickpeas with some of the reserved liquid in which they were cooked. Dice the tomatoes, discarding the seeds, and add together with the fresh sage. Add salt and pepper to taste. Then heat the mixture to absorb the seasoning. Sauté the orecchiette in the skillet. Remove from the burner, and finish with a drizzle of extra virgin olive oil. (If the pasta is too dry, add some of the salted water.) Serve the orecchiette in warmed plates garnished with the whole prawns.

Salt Cod, Chickpeas, Rosemary

▼

Preparation Time: 6 hours, plus 12 hours to soak the chickpeas

Ingredients for 6 Servings

For the Chickpea Focaccia:
3½ cups chickpea flour
1 cup extra virgin olive oil
(preferably from Apulia)
Salt and pepper
4 sprigs rosemary

For the Chickpeas:
1½ cups dried chickpeas
2 bay leaves
3 tablespoons
extra virgin olive oil
(preferably from Apulia)
3½ oz. bacon
2 sprigs rosemary
2 cloves garlic
Salt

For the Chard:
1½ lbs. young chard
4 tablespoons
extra virgin olive oil
(preferably from Apulia)
1 clove garlic
Salt

For the Salt Cod:
2 lbs. fillets of dry salt cod
1½ cups semolina flour
4 tablespoons extra virgin
olive oil
1 clove garlic
3 sprigs rosemary
Salt and pepper

Preparation

The Chickpea Focaccia: Place the chickpea flour in a bowl. Add 1½ quarts of water and half the extra virgin olive oil a little at a time, while beating with a whisk to keep the batter from getting lumpy. Mix well until the batter has the consistency of cream (if it becomes too thick, add a little water). Add salt and pepper, and let rest for at least 5 hours. Then skim off the scum that will have formed on top of the mixture, and stir in most of the remaining olive oil. Pour the mixture into a sheet pan, greased with the rest of the olive oil. Chop up the rosemary leaves, and sprinkle them over the dough. Place in a preheated 475°F oven, and bake until golden brown.

The Chickpeas: Soak the chickpeas in lukewarm water for about 12 hours. Drain, place in a sauce pan, and add lightly salted water to cover. Add the bay leaves, bring to a simmer and cook over moderate heat until the chickpeas are tender. Drain and place in a bowl. Dice the bacon, and sauté in a skillet in the extra virgin olive oil until crispy. Add the garlic cloves, whole, and the sprigs of rosemary. Sauté until the garlic is golden. Discard the garlic and rosemary. Pour the seasoned oil together with the bacon over the chickpeas. Keep in a warm place.

The Chard: Clean off and wash the chard. Discard the tough stalks, and finely slice only the tender ones and the green parts. Combine the extra virgin olive oil and the clove of garlic, whole, in a skillet, and heat until the seasoning is absorbed (the garlic must subsequently be discarded). Add the chard, and sauté until wilted. Add salt to taste. Keep warm in a strainer, so they can drain.

The Salt Cod: Cut the salt-cod fillets into pieces of equal size. Dry with paper towels and coat with semolina flour. Combine the extra virgin olive oil with the garlic clove and rosemary in a nonstick skillet and heat. As soon as the oil becomes piping hot, discard the garlic and rosemary. Brown the salt cod for about 4 minutes on both sides; let drain, and dry with paper towels.

To Serve: Cut the focaccia with a 4-inch, round pastry cutter. Place the disks in the middle of each plate; top with the chard and then with the salt cod. Spoon the chickpeas on top and finish with a little extra virgin olive oil.

Sweet Chickpea Gnocchi, Honey, Oranges

▼

Preparation Time: 1 hour

Ingredients for 6 Servings

For the Sweet Chickpea Gnocchi:
1¾ cups chickpea flour
1¾ cups white flour
6 eggs
6 tablespoons extra virgin olive oil (preferably from Apulia)
¼ cup sugar
1 quart corn oil
Salt

For the Sauce:
¾ cup orange-blossom honey
2 tablespoons orange liqueur (Grand Marnier or Cointreau)
⅔ cup almonds
6 oranges

Preparation

The Sweet Chickpea Gnocchi: Combine the two types of flour in a bowl and mix together. Place the mixture on a clean surface, and make a well in the middle. Place 6 egg yolks, 3 egg whites (the remaining egg whites will be used later), the extra virgin olive oil, sugar, and a dash of salt in the well. Mix the ingredients little by little with a fork. Knead the mixture with your hands until the dough is well blended but not too stiff. Flour the work surface. Roll the dough in cylinders of ⅜ inch diameter; then cut with a spatula in ⅜-inch-long gnocchi. Deep-fry in the corn oil until golden brown. Drain and dry on paper towels. Keep in a warm place.

The Sauce: Toast the almonds in a preheated 350°F oven for about 10 minutes. Let cool, and chop finely. Cut the orange rinds into very thin strips (be sure to discard the white part that has a bitter taste). Blanch in boiling water, rinse in cold water, and let dry. Melt the orange-blossom honey with the liqueur in a double boiler.

To Serve: Place the gnocchi in the middle of the plates, pour some of the warm honey on top, sprinkle with chopped almonds, and finish with thin strips of orange rind.

BASILICATA

Rosemary

SCALLOPS, BEANS, ROSEMARY OLIVE OIL

▼

Preparation Time: 1 hour, plus 2 hours to season the oil and 6 hours to soak the beans

Ingredients for 4 Servings

For the Beans:
1½ cups dried beans
½ onion
½ carrot
½ celery stalk
2 cloves garlic
3 tablespoons extra virgin olive oil
Salt and pepper

For the Rosemary Olive Oil:
4 sprigs rosemary
¾ cup extra virgin olive oil

For the Scallops:
1 sprig rosemary
4 tablespoons bread crumbs
16 large scallops
3 tablespoons extra virgin olive oil
Salt and pepper

For the Garnish:
4 sprigs young rosemary

Preparation

The Beans: Soak the beans in lukewarm water for about 6 hours. Meanwhile, slice the vegetables, combine with the whole garlic cloves in a pot, and brown in 3 tablespoons of the extra virgin olive oil. Drain the beans, stir them into the pot, and add water to cover. Cook until tender (if they get too dry, add more water). With a slotted spoon remove about half the cooked beans. Reserve some of the cooking liquid. Discard the garlic cloves, and put the remaining beans and vegetables in a blender. Blend until the mixture is creamy. Add salt and pepper to taste, and combine with the whole beans that were set aside. Cook the mixture over moderate heat for about 2 minutes. Keep in a warm place.

The Rosemary Olive Oil: Remove the rosemary leaves from the stems, and chop them in a food processor. Add the olive oil, and leave to infuse for at least 2 hours.

For the Scallops: Finely chop the rosemary leaves, and mix them with the bread crumbs. Carefully remove the scallops from their shells, and wash them in cold running water. Pat dry, and coat with the bread crumbs. Brown in the extra virgin olive oil over high heat in a nonstick skillet for about 1 minute on both sides. Add salt and pepper.

To Serve: Adjust the consistency of the bean mixture by adding the rosemary olive oil (and some of the cooking liquid, if necessary). Add salt to taste. Place the bean purée on plates, add the scallops, and garnish with a sprig of young rosemary.

GREEN TAGLIATELLE, RABBIT, ROSEMARY, BLACK OLIVES

▼

Preparation Time: 2 hours

Ingredients for 4 Servings

For the Sauce:
4 rabbit legs, with thighs

5 San Marzano tomatoes (or Roma tomatoes)

2 shallots

3½ oz. bacon

3 tablespoons extra virgin olive oil

½ cup dry white wine

4 sprigs rosemary

½ cup black olives, pitted

¾ cup freshly grated Parmesan cheese

Salt and pepper

For the Green Tagliatelle Dough:
1 cup spinach leaves

2¼ cups flour

2 eggs

Salt

Preparation

The Sauce: Bone the rabbit legs, and finely chop the meat with a knife. Blanch the tomatoes in boiling water, remove, and place in ice water to stop the cooking process. Peel and dice, discarding the seeds. Peel and finely chop the shallots. Dice the bacon, and cook over moderate heat in a skillet. Discard the bacon grease as soon as it is rendered. Add the shallots and 2 tablespoons of the extra virgin olive oil. Brown. Sauté the rabbit meat in the remaining olive oil in another nonstick skillet for about 2 minutes. Remove the meat from the skillet, and combine with the bacon. Add the wine, let evaporate, and then stir in the tomatoes, the finely chopped rosemary leaves, and the pitted olives. Simmer for 10 minutes. Add salt and pepper. Mix well and remove from the heat. Keep in a warm place.

The Green Tagliatelle: Clean, wash, blanch, and drain the spinach leaves. Squeeze dry in a kitchen cloth. Chop them in a food processor. Mix the spinach with the eggs and prepare the pasta dough (see Basic Recipes). Roll out a thin sheet of dough on a clean, smooth surface, and let dry slightly. Shape the tagliatelle (see Basic Recipes). Cook them in plenty of salted water, and drain while still slightly underdone.

To Serve: Sauté the green tagliatelle in a skillet together with the rabbit sauce. Mix well and serve on warmed plates topped with the grated Parmesan cheese.

Sea Bream, Pancetta, Rosemary

—————————▼—————————

Preparation Time: 45 minutes

Ingredients for 4 Servings

For the Flavored Oil:
6 cloves garlic
8 sprigs rosemary
1 cup extra virgin olive oil

For the Sea Bream:
4 sea bream of 1 lb. each, cleaned
4 bay leaves
8 slices pancetta
Salt and pepper

Preparation

The Flavored Oil: Finely chop 2 garlic cloves with the leaves of 4 rosemary sprigs, combine with the extra virgin olive oil, mix well, and set aside for 20 minutes.

The Sea Bream: Salt the insides of the fish. Place 1 garlic clove, 1 rosemary sprig, and a bay leaf in each. Wrap each sea bream in 2 slices of bacon, and tie with a string. Now brush both sides with the flavored olive oil. Broil the fish for about 15 minutes, turning them carefully several times.

To Serve: Remove the strings from the sea bream, add salt and pepper to taste, and serve on individual plates, drizzling with the flavored olive oil.

ROSEMARY-FLAVORED BISCOTTI

Preparation Time: 1 hour

Ingredients for 12 Servings

Rosemary-Flavored Biscotti:

1½ cups almonds
8 cups flour
8 eggs
½ teaspoon baking powder
½ teaspoon baking soda
3 cups sugar
½ oz. fresh rosemary leaves
Salt

Preparation

The Rosemary-Flavored Biscotti: Blanch the almonds, peel, and dry by placing in the oven for a few minutes. Place the flour on a thoroughly clean surface, and make a well in the middle. Place the eggs, baking powder, baking soda, sugar, the finely chopped rosemary leaves, and a dash of salt in the well, mix in, and knead the dough. Add the almonds, and continue to knead. Shape the dough into 1½-inch rolls. Place on a cookie sheet lined with wax paper, and bake in a preheated 300°F oven for about 15 minutes. Remove the rolls from the oven, and cut on the diagonal into biscotti with a ⅜-inch diameter. Put them back into the oven for another 10 minutes to finish baking. Let cool.

To Serve: Place rosemary-flavored biscotti on a tray, and serve with a glass of dessert wine with a sherrylike character.

CALABRIA

Fig

CHICKEN LIVERS, FIGS

Preparation Time: 1 hour

Ingredients for 4 Servings

For the Sauce:
2 shallots
⅓ cup butter
4 ripe figs
2 cups dry red wine
Salt and pepper

For the Chicken Livers:
32 chicken livers
2 bay leaves
½ cup butter
Salt and pepper
2 tablespoons Stravecchio brandy

Preparation

The Sauce: Clean the shallots, and chop very fine. Sauté the shallots in the butter in a skillet until golden brown. Peel the figs, and add to the shallots. Add the red wine, and cook until the wine is reduced by half. Season to taste with salt and pepper. Remove from the burner, and keep in a warm place.

The Chicken Livers: Wash the livers in running water, drain, and pat dry. Carefully remove the bile and the veins. Brown them with the bay leaves in a nonstick skillet, using ¼ cup of the butter. When the chicken livers are pink on the inside, season with salt and pepper and remove from the skillet. Keep in a warm place. Add the Stravecchio brandy to the cooking juices, and let it evaporate. Add the fig sauce, and cook until reduced by half. Stir the rest of the butter into the mixture and put through a medium-mesh strainer. Add salt to taste.

To Serve: Serve the hot chicken livers with the fig sauce on individual plates.

FARFALLE, PIGEON, FIGS

▼

Preparation Time: 2 hours, plus 12 hours for the marinade

Ingredients for 4 Servings

For the Sauce:
2 pigeons
½ celery stalk
½ onion
2 cups dry red wine
2 tablespoons sugar
4 black figs
Salt and pepper
⅓ cup butter
2 tablespoons extra virgin olive oil

For the Farfalle:
11 oz. farfalle (bow-tie pasta)
Salt

Preparation

The Sauce: Quarter the pigeons. Bone the breasts, and place in a cool place together with the legs and thighs. Chop the celery and onion and place in a container with the bones and red wine. Marinate for about 12 hours. Then put the marinade in a large pot on the burner, bring to a boil, and cook until the wine is reduced by half. Add enough water to bring the liquid up to the original level, and cook until reduced by two-thirds. Put the pigeon stock through a fine-mesh strainer and set aside. Place the sugar in a nonstick skillet, and dissolve with a little water. Dice the figs, add to the sugar mixture, and coat them on all sides. Add them to the pigeon stock, and cook for about 15 minutes. Strain the mixture through a medium-mesh sieve, making sure that the mashed figs go through. Season the pigeon breasts, legs, and thighs with salt and pepper. Combine half the butter with the extra virgin olive oil in a skillet, and brown the meat. Add the pigeon stock, and cook until the meat is tender but still pink on the inside. Remove the pigeon, bone the legs and thighs, and dice all the meat into small pieces. Place the skillet with the stock back on the burner, and stir in the meat and remaining butter. Heat for a few minutes to let the meat absorb the seasoning. Add salt and pepper to taste. Keep warm.

The Farfalle: Cook the farfalle in plenty of salted water, and drain while slightly underdone.

To Serve: Sauté the pasta in the skillet together with the pigeon-and-fig sauce. Serve on warmed plates.

CATFISH, GRAPE LEAVES, FIGS, LEMON

▼

Preparation Time: 45 minutes

Ingredients for 4 Servings

For the Sauce:
6 ripe figs
⅓ cup butter
Juice of 1 lemon

For the Catfish:
1 catfish, 3 to 3½ lbs., cleaned
Salt and pepper
6 grape leaves
5 tablespoons corn oil
¼ cup butter
⅓ cup flour

Preparation

The Sauce: Wash and dice the unpeeled figs. Melt the butter in a nonstick skillet, add the figs, and cook over moderate heat for about 3 minutes. Add the lemon juice and mix well. Remove from the burner, and keep in a warm place.

The Catfish: Season the catfish on the inside and outside with salt and pepper. Blanch the grape leaves, and wrap them around the fish. Heat the corn oil and the butter in a nonstick skillet; dust the fish in flour, and brown over moderate heat until golden brown on both sides.

To Serve: Serve the fish whole on a platter together with the fig sauce.

FIG TART, CHOCOLATE SORBET

▼

Preparation Time: 90 minutes

Ingredients for 8 Servings

For the Short Pastry:
1½ cups flour
1 egg
1 lemon
½ cup sugar
⅓ cup butter
1 teaspoon baking powder

For the Fig Tart:
1 lemon
¼ cup sugar
2¼ lbs. ripe figs

For the Chocolate Sorbet:
5 oz. semi-sweet chocolate
¾ cup sugar
1¼ cups unsweetened cocoa

Preparation

The Short Pastry: Prepare short pastry dough (see Basic Recipes). Roll it out on a clean surface with a lightly floured rolling pin until it is about ⅛ inch thick. Place the pastry in a 10-inch cake pan and press it evenly against the sides. Set aside.

The Fig Tart: Wash the lemon and cut it in thin slices. Sauté the slices in a nonstick skillet for about 10 minutes with the sugar and ½ cup of water. Remove the slices with a spatula, and distribute them over the pastry shell. Set the syrup aside. Slice the figs, and place them in overlapping layers on top of the lemon slices. Drizzle the syrup over the fruit. Bake the tart in a preheated 350°F oven for about 30 minutes. Remove from the oven and let cool.

The Chocolate Sorbet: Melt the semi-sweet chocolate in a double boiler. Bring ½ quart of water to a boil in a saucepan, and add the sugar, the powdered cocoa, and the melted chocolate. Mix well. Remove from the burner, and strain the mixture through a fine-mesh sieve. Let cool; then pour into an ice-cream machine.

To Serve: Slice the tart, and serve on individual plates together with a heaping spoonful of the chocolate sorbet.

SICILY

Orange

CRAB, OREGANO, BLACK OLIVES, ORANGES

▼

Preparation Time: 90 minutes

Ingredients for 4 Servings

For the Crab:
1 carrot
1 onion
1 stalk celery
Salt
1 sprig thyme
4 bay leaves
2 sprigs parsley
4 medium-sized crabs

For the Sauce:
¾ cup black olives
2 oranges
1 lemon
½ cup extra virgin olive oil
Salt
1 clove garlic
1 teaspoon dried oregano

For the Garnish:
2 oranges
3½ oz mâche

Preparation

The Crab: Dice the vegetables and place in a pot. Add lightly salted water, and prepare a broth with the thyme, bay leaves, and parsley. Bring to a boil, and then add the crabs, whole. Cook for about 10 to 15 minutes, depending on their size. Drain and let cool. Remove the meat from the legs and the body. Set aside.

The Sauce: Pit the olives, and cut them in half. Wash the oranges and grate the rinds, being careful not to use the white part since it has a bitter taste. Squeeze the juice from the oranges and from the lemon. Combine it in a bowl with the extra virgin olive oil. Add salt to taste and emulsify well. Gently squeeze, but keep whole, the garlic clove, and add to the mixture. Also add the olives, oregano, and grated orange rinds. Mix and then let rest for half an hour. Be sure to remove the garlic before serving.

The Garnish: Julienne the orange rinds, being careful not to use the white part with the bitter taste. Blanch, rinse in running water, and dry with a kitchen cloth. Take the orange wedges and remove the thin skin around each. Clean, wash and dry the mâche.

To Serve: Place the crabmeat on individual plates, and top with some of the sauce. Garnish with the orange sections and a little mâche.

RICOTTA-CHEESE PANZOTTI, LEMONS, ORANGES

▼

Preparation Time: 90 minutes

Ingredients for 6 Servings

For the Filling:
1 lemon
1 orange
2 cups ricotta cheese
2 eggs
1 cup freshly grated
Parmesan cheese
Nutmeg
Salt and pepper

For the Garnish:
1 lemon
1 orange

For the Sauce:
1 lemon
1 orange
½ cup butter
1 cup grated Parmesan cheese

For the Panzotti Dough:
3¾ cups flour
5 eggs (1 egg will be used
to seal them)
Salt

Preparation

The Filling: Grate the rinds of the lemon and the orange, being careful not to use the white part since it has a bitter taste. Put the ricotta cheese through a sieve and place in a bowl. Add the egg yolks, grated Parmesan cheese, half the grated rinds (reserve the other half for the sauce), and a dash of nutmeg. Season with salt and pepper to taste.

The Garnish: Cut the lemon and orange rinds into fine julienne (being careful not to use the white part, which has a bitter taste), and blanch in boiling water for about 3 minutes. Drain, rinse in cold running water, and set aside.

The Sauce: Pour ½ cup of water in a skillet, and add the butter, reserved grated rinds, 1 tablespoon of orange juice, and 1 tablespoon of lemon juice. Heat until reduced by half. Keep warm.

The Ricotta-Cheese Panzotti: Roll out a thin sheet of dough, and prepare the panzotti (see Basic Recipes). Then cook in plenty of salted water and drain carefully, reserving some of the water.

To Serve: Pour the citrus-flavored sauce in a skillet, and sauté the panzotti (if the pasta should become too dry, add a little of the salted water). Serve hot on individual plates, topping with the sauce and sprinkling with some grated Parmesan cheese. Garnish with the citrus-rind strips.

TURBOT, RED ONIONS, FENNEL, ORANGES

▼

Preparation Time: 1 hour

Ingredients for 4 Servings

For the Sauce:
2 large red onions
1 medium-sized fennel
4 tablespoons extra virgin olive oil
1 clove garlic
1 tablespoon red wine vinegar
1 tablespoon honey
1 orange
2 tablespoons butter
Salt and pepper

For the Turbot:
2 turbots, 2 to 2½ lbs. each, cleaned
½ quart vegetable stock (see Basic Recipes)
1 bouquet garni (see Basic Recipes)
Salt

For the Garnish:
Extra virgin olive oil

Preparation

The Sauce: Slice the onions and fennel, discarding the tough outer layers. Heat the extra virgin olive oil, and brown the whole garlic clove over high heat. Add the onions. Cook for about 5 minutes. Now add the fennel, vinegar, honey, and the juice of one-half orange. Cook for two more minutes, and thicken with the butter. Season with salt and pepper to taste, and keep in a warm place.

The Turbot: Wash the turbots and cut them into fillets. Place the fillets on a baking pan, and pour the hot vegetable stock over them. Add salt to taste and the bouquet garni, and cook in a preheated 375° to 400°F oven for about 10 minutes, making sure that the stock never reaches the boiling point.

To Serve: Put some of the onion sauce on each plate, and place the turbot fillets on top. Finish by drizzling some extra virgin olive oil over them.

SEMIFREDDO WITH TORRONE NOUGAT, ORANGES

▼

Preparation Time: 1 hour, plus 2 hours to freeze

Ingredients for 4 Servings

For the Semifreddo with Torrone Nougat:

7 oz. torrone nougat

1 cup heavy cream

4 eggs

½ cup sugar

For the Orange Sauce:

1 teaspoon cornstarch

4 oranges

⅓ cup sugar

4 tablespoons orange liqueur (Grand Marnier or Cointreau)

½ cup dry spumante wine

For the Candied Orange Rinds:

½ cup candied orange rinds

(It takes a few days to prepare candied orange rinds from fresh oranges; we describe their preparation in the Basic Recipes.)

Preparation

The Semifreddo with Torrone Nougat: Finely chop the torrone nougat. Whip the cream. Beat the egg whites until very stiff, and beat the yolks with the sugar. Begin by mixing the yolks into the whipped cream, and then add the egg whites. Blend the torrone nougat carefully into the mixture, and pour it into 2½-inch ring-shaped moulds about 1 inch deep. Place them in the freezer and let cool for about 2 hours.

The Orange Sauce: Mix the cornstarch with a tablespoon of cold water. Squeeze the oranges. Put all the ingredients in a saucepan, and cook until reduced to one-fourth of the volume. Remove from the burner and let cool.

To Serve: Place the semifreddo on individual plates by turning the moulds upside down over the plates. Top with the orange sauce and thin strips of the candied rinds.

SARDINIA

Honey

TROUT, MUSTARD, HONEY

▼

Preparation Time: 1 hour, plus 24 hours for the marinade

Ingredients for 4 Servings

For the Cured Trout:
2 tablespoons salt
½ tablespoon sugar
Pepper
2 sprigs dill
4 medium-sized trout
1 tablespoon wine brandy (regional name: *filu 'e ferru*)

For the Sauce:
1 sprig dill
1 egg yolk
1 lemon
2 tablespoons mustard
1 tablespoon honey
4 tablespoons corn oil

Preparation

The Cured Trout: Mix the salt and sugar in a bowl, and add a dash of pepper. Finely chop the dill. Wash the trout in running water, and open them up halfway by cutting along the belly and leaving the back intact. Gut them, discarding the bones, heads, and tails. Place them open and skin side down in a glass pan of the right size. Sprinkle the brine evenly over the fish; do the same with the dill and then with the brandy. Close them up again. Place the glass dish in the refrigerator, and let the trout marinate for 24 hours.

For the Sauce: Finely chop the dill. Squeeze the juice from the lemon. Now blend all the ingredients in a blender until the mixture is well blended.

To Serve: Remove the remnants of the marinade from the trout fillets, place them on individual plates and add a little of the sauce.

Semolina, Honey, Salt

Preparation Time: 45 minutes

Ingredients for 4 Servings

For the Semolina Polenta:
2¼ cups fine semolina
Salt

For the Sauce:
8 tablespoons honey
8 tablespoons salt

Preparation

The Semolina Polenta: Boil lightly salted water in a deep saucepan. Add the semolina little by little, very slowly while beating with a whisk. Stirring constantly with a wooden spoon, cook over low heat for about 20 minutes or until the polenta reaches a creamy consistency. (If the mixture should become too dry, add more boiling water.)

To Serve: Serve the semolina polenta in deep plates. Serve the honey and the salt as side dishes, to be used as desired according to individual taste.

PORK, HONEY, MYRTLE

▼

Preparation Time: 4 hours

Ingredients for 10 Servings

For the Glaze:
⅔ cup honey
½ quart extra virgin olive oil
½ cup Vernaccia wine (a white table wine from Sardinia)
3 sprigs myrtle

For the Pork:
1 suckling pig, with the liver, about 10 lbs.
½ cup lard
2 cloves garlic
6 sprigs myrtle
2 sprigs sage
Salt

Preparation

The Glaze: Place all the ingredients in a blender, and blend until the mixture is well blended.

The Pork: Have the butcher bone the suckling pig. Wash the pig and scrape the skin well. Place the liver in a blender, and add the lard, garlic cloves, and the myrtle and sage leaves. Process the ingredients until the mixture is well blended. Add salt to taste. Spread the mixture on the insides of the pig, tie it together well with a thin string, and sprinkle it on the outside with lots of salt. Put the pig on a spit (or in a baking pan), and bake it in a moderately hot oven for about 3 hours or until it becomes a dark, golden brown. While baking, brush the skin frequently with the honey glaze.

To Serve: Cut the pig in ¾-inch slices, and serve on warm plates.

Honey Cake, Honey Semifreddo

▼

Preparation Time: 2 hours, plus 1 hour to let the dough rise and 4 hours for freezing

Ingredients for 4 Servings

For the Cake:
½ oz. yeast (1 envelope dry yeast)
1 cup milk
2 tablespoons sugar
1 vanilla bean
1¾ cups flour
¼ cup butter
1 lemon
Salt

For the Honey Layer:
2 tablespoons honey
3 tablespoons heavy cream
¾ cup butter
1½ cup shelled walnuts, coarsely chopped

For the Honey Semifreddo:
5 eggs
½ cup sugar
1 tablespoon orange-blossom honey
1 vanilla bean
½ quart heavy cream

Preparation

The Cake Dough: Dissolve the yeast in ½ cup lukewarm milk. Add the sugar and vanilla bean (sliced open lengthwise). Place the flour on a smooth, clean surface, and make a well in the middle, into which you place the butter, the milk and yeast mixture, the seeds of the vanilla bean, the grated lemon rind (being careful not to use the white bitter part), and a dash of salt. Mix all the ingredients little by little with the help of a fork. Then knead the dough with your hands until it becomes elastic. Let the dough rise for about 1 hour in a somewhat warm place.

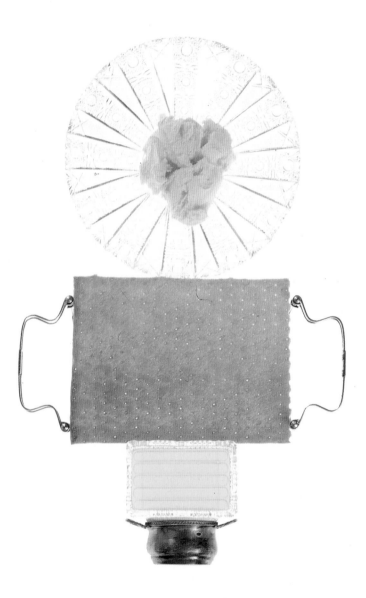

The Honey Layer: Place the honey, heavy cream, and butter in a saucepan, and cook over moderate heat for a few minutes. Then add the coarsely chopped walnuts.

The Honey Cake: Grease an 8-inch cake pan and dust with flour. Knead the dough a few more minutes after it has risen; then roll it out and fit it into the cake pan. Spread the honey layer onto the dough so that it is distributed evenly. Bake in a preheated 350°F oven for about 30 minutes. Remove from the oven and let cool.

The Honey Semifreddo: Combine the egg yolks with the sugar in a saucepan and mix well. Add the honey and the seeds of the vanilla bean (sliced open lengthwise). Cook the mixture in a double boiler, beating with a whisk until the mixture becomes smooth and firm. Remove from the heat, and stir constantly until cool. Whip the heavy cream, and fold it carefully into the mixture. Place in the freezer.

To Serve: Cut the honey cake into slices, and serve on individual plates together with a heaping spoonful of the honey semifreddo.

BASIC RECIPES

FISH STOCK

▼

Preparation Time: 1 hour

Ingredients:
1½ lbs. fish bones
1 onion
1 carrot
1 celery stalk
5 tablespoons extra virgin olive oil
1 bouquet garni (see page 215)
Salt and whole black peppercorns
1 quart water

Preparation

Wash the bones. Clean and dice the vegetables. Brown the vegetables in the extra virgin olive oil in a large skillet. Add the fish bones, bouquet garni, and peppercorns. Cook about 7 minutes. Add salt to taste. Then add 1 quart of cold water, and bring to a boil. Cook for about 30 minutes, skimming the scum off frequently. When finished cooking, strain the stock through a fine-mesh sieve.

FISH BROTH

▼

Preparation Time: 1 hour

Ingredients:
1½ lbs. fish bones
1 onion
1 celery stalk
5 mushroom caps
1 bouquet garni (see page 215)
1 quart water

Preparation

Wash the bones. Clean and dice the vegetables. Place all the ingredients in a pan with cold water, and bring to a boil. Cook for about 40 minutes, skimming the scum off frequently. When finished cooking, strain the broth through a fine-mesh sieve.

VEGETABLE STOCK

▼

Preparation Time: 75 minutes

Ingredients:
2 carrots
2 stalks celery
1 onion
1½ quarts water
Salt

Preparation

Clean and wash the vegetables. Place in a pan with cold water, and bring to a boil. Cook for about 1 hour, and add salt to taste. When finished cooking, strain the stock through a fine-mesh sieve.

CHICKEN STOCK

▼

Preparation Time: 90 minutes

Ingredients:
1 medium-sized chicken, cleaned
1 onion
1 carrot
1 celery stalk
Coarse salt

Preparation

Clean and wash the chicken and the vegetables. Place all the ingredients in a pan with cold, lightly salted water, and bring to a boil. Cook for about 1 hour, skimming the scum off frequently. When finished cooking, strain the stock through a fine-mesh sieve.

VEAL STOCK

▼

Preparation Time: 8 hours

Ingredients:
2 carrots
2 onions
4 tomatoes
6½ lbs. veal bones (preferably hocks)
1 bouquet garni
1 tablespoon tomato paste

Preparation

Clean, wash, and dice the vegetables. Break the bones into small pieces, place them on a baking pan, and bake in a preheated 475°F oven for about 40 minutes or until they are thoroughly baked. Remove from the oven, and place in a pot together with the vegetables, bouquet garni, and tomato paste. Fill the pot with water to twice the height of the ingredients. Cook slowly for about 6 hours, skimming the scum off frequently. Add more water as the level of the water goes down. Let the stock sit for a while after it is finished cooking, and then strain through a fine-mesh sieve. The stock can be kept in the refrigerator for several weeks if desired.

DUCK STOCK

▼

Preparation Time: 4 hours

Ingredients:

1 carrot   *1 duck carcass*
1 onion   *1 bouquet garni*
1 stalk celery

Preparation

Clean, wash, and dice the vegetables. Break the duck bones into small pieces, place on a baking pan, and cook in a preheated 475°F oven for about 40 minutes or until golden brown. Remove them from the oven, and place in a pot together with the vegetables and bouquet garni. Fill the pot with water and bring to a boil, and then simmer for about 3 hours, skimming the scum off frequently. Add more water as the level of the water goes down. Let the stock sit for a while after it is finished cooking, and then strain through a fine-mesh sieve.

BOUQUET GARNI

▼

Preparation Time: 5 minutes

Ingredients for 1 bouquet:

3 thyme sprigs   *10 parsley sprigs*
1 bay leaf   *5 celery leaves*

Preparation

Tie all the herbs together with a thin string.

RISOTTO

Preparation Time: 30 minutes

Ingredients:

Stock	Dry white wine
Onion	Butter
Extra virgin olive oil	½ cup freshly grated
Small-grain rice (Carnaroli,	Parmesan cheese
Vialone Nano, or Arborio)	Salt (optional)

Preparation

Simmer the stock in a separate pan. Finely chop the onion, and brown in the extra virgin olive oil in a saucepan. Add the rice and heat for about 2 minutes, stirring with a wooden spoon. Add the wine and let evaporate. Cook the rice until done (18 to 20 minutes), adding the simmering stock a little at a time, so it barely covers the liquid. When the rice is cooked, remove from the burner. Add the butter and the Parmesan cheese, and stir continuously until it becomes creamy.

PASTA DOUGH

Preparation Time: 30 minutes

Ingredients:

Flour

Eggs

Preparation

Place the flour on a smooth, thoroughly clean surface, and make a well in the middle. Place the eggs in the well, and mix them into the flour a little at a time with the help of a fork. Then knead until the dough has a smooth and even consistency. Roll the dough out with a lightly floured rolling pin or run it through a pasta machine to make thin sheets about ⅛-inch thick.

TORTELLI, TORTELLONI, AND CAPPELLACCI

▼

Cut the pasta sheet in small squares of about 1½ inches for the tortelli, 2¼ inches for the tortelloni, and 3 inches for the cappellacci. Brush with egg wash (equal quantities of egg yolk and water). Place a teaspoon of the filling (2 heaping teaspoons for the cappellacci) in the middle of each square until all the filling is used up. Fold the dough into triangles, and seal by pressing down on the edges with your fingers. Fold the corners at the base of the triangle around your left index finger and press them firmly together between your right thumb and index finger.

RAVIOLI AND PANZOTTI

▼

Spread half the pasta sheets on a clean surface. Place small amounts of filling (about a teaspoon) about 1 inch apart from each other on the dough, until all the filling is used up. Cover with the remaining sheets of dough, and seal with your fingers around the filling. For square-shaped ravioli, cut them with a serrated pastry cutter. For half-moon shapes, cut the dough into small disks with the appropriate pastry cutter, place a small amount of the filling in the middle, and seal by overlapping the edges.

TAGLIOLINI, TAGLIATELLE, FETTUCCINE, PAPPARDELLE, AND MALTAGLIATI PASTA

▼

Let the rolled dough dry slightly, sprinkle it with flour, and roll it up loosely. Slice the roll into strips: ¼ inch for the tagliolini, ⅜ inch for the tagliatelle, ½ inch for the fettuccine, and ¾ inch for the pappardelle. For the maltagliati, cut into irregularly shaped rhombuses. Open the little rolls of pasta carefully with your hands, and spread them out on a clean cloth to dry.

POLENTA

▼

Preparation Time: 45 minutes

Ingredients:

Water

Salt

Extra virgin olive oil

Cornmeal used for polenta
(fine-grained)

(It is very difficult to indicate the exact amount of water required, since it depends on the different qualities of cornmeal used. However, for a rather solid polenta, about 1½ quarts of water are needed for each 3⅓ cups of cornmeal; for a softer polenta, use about 1¾ quarts of water.)

Preparation

Place a large, deep pan (preferably made of copper) on the stove with about 1 quart of lightly salted water and the extra virgin olive oil. Bring to a boil. Add the cornmeal little by little and very slowly, beating with a whisk. Cook over moderate heat for about 45 minutes or until the consistency of the polenta becomes creamy, stirring constantly with a wooden spoon. Add salt to taste.

TOMATO SAUCE

▼

Preparation Time: 1 hour

Ingredients:

2¼ lbs ripe San Marzano tomatoes (or Roma tomatoes)

1 onion

½ carrot

½ stalk celery

½ cup extra virgin olive oil

1 clove garlic

4 basil leaves

Preparation

Wash the tomatoes and chop them coarsely, discarding the seeds. Wash the vegetables and dice them very fine. In a skillet, brown the vegetables and the garlic clove in the extra virgin olive oil for about 7 minutes over moderate heat. Add the tomatoes and cook for about 30 minutes. Remove from the fire, add the basil leaves, and pass through a food mill.

CANDIED ORANGE RINDS

▼

Preparation Time: about 6 days

Ingredients:
2 oranges
5¼ cups sugar

Preparation

Peel the oranges, and cut the rinds in fine julienne. Fill a saucepan with water, and bring to a boil. Place the orange rinds in the saucepan, and cook until they are tender. Drain, let them drip dry, and then let them sit in a bowl with cold water for two hours. Drain and let drip dry once more. Scrape the white part off, rinse again, and dry well with a kitchen cloth. Heat the sugar and 1½ quarts of water in a pan, and stir until the sugar is completely dissolved. Add the orange rinds, and let the liquid boil for a few minutes. Remove from the burner, and let the mixture cool in a bowl. The next day, bring only the syrup to a boil, and heat a few minutes to reduce it. Stir in the orange rinds again, and let them cook for a few more minutes. Remove from the burner, and let the mixture cool again in a bowl. Repeat the same procedure after two days, let rest again for 48 hours, and repeat the procedure again for the last time. Drain the orange rinds; place them on a cookie sheet to dry in a well-ventilated area.

VANILLA ICE CREAM

▼

Preparation Time: 1 hour

Ingredients:
½ quart milk	*12 eggs*
½ quart heavy cream	*1¼ cups sugar*
4 vanilla beans	

Preparation

Combine the milk and cream in a saucepan, and add the vanilla beans, cut open lengthwise. Place the saucepan on the stove and bring to a boil. Whip the egg yolks with the sugar with a whisk. Add the milk and cream mixture very slowly. Blend well. Heat again, but do not bring to a boil. Cook the mixture until it coats a spoon. Let cool, strain through a fine-mesh sieve (after discarding the vanilla beans), and place in an ice-cream machine.

Cooked Wine

▼

Preparation Time: 3 hours

Ingredients:
4½ lbs light or dark grapes

Preparation

Wash the grape clusters, remove the grapes from the stalks, and squeeze the juice into a nonreactive container (ceramic, glass, or stainless steel). Filter the liquid through cheesecloth and let it cook (again, in a nonreactive container) for about 3 hours, while stirring frequently. Remove from the heat when the consistency of the mixture becomes rather thick. Let cool.

Candied Squash

▼

Preparation Time: about 6 days

Ingredients:
1 lb. butternut-squash meat
2½ cups salt
5¼ cups sugar
1 vanilla bean

Preparation

Cut the squash meat into strips, discarding the seeds. Distribute the strips over a cookie sheet that is placed at a slight angle, so that the excess water can drain from them. Completely cover them with the salt, and let rest for about 48 hours. Remove the salt from the meat by rinsing thoroughly with cool running water several times. Boil the squash meat in a pan until tender. Drain it, place it in cool water, and let it cool. Prepare a syrup by dissolving the sugar in ¾ quarts of water and adding the vanilla bean, cut open lengthwise. Remove the syrup from the burner, and add the squash meat. Let sit for 24 hours. Remove the strips of squash meat with a slotted spoon, being careful not to break them, and set aside. Bring the syrup to a boil, and let it boil for a few minutes until it thickens. Place the squash in the syrup again, leaving it there for another 24 hours. Repeat the same procedure a total of four times. The last time, drain the strips of squash meat and let them dry in a well-ventilated area.

SHORT PASTRY

▼

Preparation Time: 30 minutes

Ingredients:
Flour

Eggs

Grated lemon rind

Sugar

Butter

Baking powder

(According to the classical recipe, baking powder is normally not used for short pastry. We use it so as to produce a dough that is less rich in butter and just as crumbly.)

Preparation

Place the flour on a smooth, thoroughly clean surface, and make a well in the middle. Place the eggs and the grated lemon rind (being careful not to use the white part that has a bitter taste) in the well with all the other ingredients. Mix little by little with the help of a fork. Then knead the dough quickly with your fingertips (so as not to warm it up) until the ingredients are blended. Wrap in clear plastic wrap, and let rest about a half hour in a cool place.

Index

222

223